# B

## BOBBY FLAY'S BURGERS FRIES & SHAKES

# BOBBY FLAY'S BURGERS FRIES & SHAKES

## BOBBY FLAY
### WITH
### STEPHANIE BANYAS
### & SALLY JACKSON

PHOTOGRAPHS BY BEN FINK

CLARKSON POTTER/PUBLISHERS
NEW YORK

I dedicate this book to my most trusted employee, Stephanie Banyas.
Stephanie has demonstrated her love of food, her dedication to all we do together,
and most important her unwavering loyalty to me for almost fourteen years.
She is truly irreplaceable.

   On a side note, Stephanie has never seen a milkshake she didn't like . . .

## ALSO BY BOBBY FLAY

BOBBY FLAY'S GRILL IT!

BOBBY FLAY'S MESA GRILL COOKBOOK

BOBBY FLAY'S GRILLING FOR LIFE

BOBBY FLAY'S BOY GETS GRILL

BOBBY FLAY COOKS AMERICAN

BOBBY FLAY'S BOY MEETS GRILL

BOBBY FLAY'S FROM MY KITCHEN TO YOUR TABLE

BOBBY FLAY'S BOLD AMERICAN FOOD

# CONTENTS

INTRODUCTION 6

BURGERS 8

FRENCH FRIES, POTATO CHIPS, AND ONION RINGS 80

CONDIMENTS AND SEASONINGS 102

MILKSHAKES 120

RESOURCES AND ACKNOWLEDGMENTS 156

INDEX 157

# INTRODUCTION

I think it's fair to say that most people are under the assumption that when it comes time for me to eat, whether I'm cooking for myself or going out, my taste must be pretty extravagant: foie gras, caviar, fine dining with five-course meals and linen napkins—you get the picture. And while I certainly can appreciate meals such as those, I promise you that it is not what goes on in my house or goes into my stomach on a daily or even weekly basis. Turkey sandwiches, salads, sushi, a slice of pizza here and there, maybe some tacos—these are my lunchtime staples. And my all-time favorite meal—the one that satisfies any hunger—is a cheeseburger with fries and a shake. Done right, it doesn't get much better than that.

I've been eating burgers for as long as I can remember. I started the way most kids in America start eating burgers—at a local fast-food place. But that didn't last long for me. I was soon exposed to something better.

In New York City, where I grew up and continue to live today, my memories include a place called Jackson Hole, where the burgers were oversized and juicy and crusty on the outside. It was the first place I remember being able to order toppings like sautéed mushrooms and cheeses other than American and cheddar. Just the fact that I could go to a place, order my burger, and watch it being cooked to order was a fundamental step up from the insta-burgers I was eating earlier on. I quickly learned that there are burgers and then there are *burgers*.

In New York City, as in most towns, the debate about who serves the best burger rages on. If you ask the locals, you'll hear cries for places like Corner Bistro downtown in the Village or the Burger Joint in Midtown or the Shake Shack in Madison Square Park. They all serve delicious and really satisfying burgers and any of them could take the crown for best burger in the city.

Personally, the place that has been my go-to since I was eight years old is a saloon on the Upper East Side called J.G. Melon. In full disclosure, I admit that the owners are friends of mine, basically family, and I love them dearly. But it's the burger that drives me and hundreds of people a day to Melon's.

Every time I go, I hear people ask themselves and their company, "What is it about these burgers that makes them so good?" The answer in my mind is simple: the meat, the griddle, and the bun. And yet, achieving the perfect burger is not.

Even as I was opening high-end, full-service restaurants, I always dreamed of opening my own burger place. I'm just like most other chefs: we all like to eat simple things—what I call late-night cuisine—and the hamburger fits prominently into that category. I often wondered what that place would be like. Would it be a sports bar? A tavern or a saloon? A diner?

I knew it had to have thick, creamy, full-flavored shakes, like the black-and-white my friend turned me on to as a kid. And of course fries, something crispy to round out the perfect casual meal of a savory cheeseburger and a silky shake. Potato chips or fries, or onion rings battered for flavor and texture.

I finally decided to open a place that's not about the game on television or the draft beer behind the bar but the meal I care about most. A place that's about burgers, fries, and shakes—an ode to the idiom.

And then one day in 2008, it was open. My burger place, with a name that I think spells it all out: Bobby's Burger Palace.

It's a place where you can order everything from a simple hamburger topped with American cheese to one with a combination of toppings with my favorite regional flavors or international ingredients. Your taste buds can transport you to that place between the two buns. It's a place where the shakes and malteds are dense and creamy, and scream their flavor intensely, where a collection of sauces and condiments help create a burger fantasy second to none.

I opened Bobby's Burger Palace to fulfill a longtime dream of being able to have my very own perfect burgers, shakes, and fries in my very own restaurant, and I got it. But just because the restaurant has moved out of my head and into reality doesn't mean that those dishes have to stay in the restaurant. I still want to prepare them at home, and I hope that you will want to treat your friends and family to the same. This book captures that dream and all of the work that went into making Bobby's Burger Palace, and makes it all accessible—every dish, to anyone, all of the time.

So grab a bunch of napkins and come along for the ride! Oh, and one more thing: please remember to melt the cheese completely!

7

# BOBBY FLAY
NEW YORK CITY

# BURGERS

PERFECT BURGERS 16 ARGENTINEAN BURGER 22
ARTHUR AVENUE BURGER 25 BISTRO BURGER 26 BUFFALO BURGER 27
BOLO BURGER 28 BREAKFAST BURGER 31 CAESAR SALAD BURGER 33
CALIFORNIA BURGER 34 CAROLINA BURGER 36 DALLAS BURGER 37
CHEYENNE BURGER 39 CRUNCHBURGER 40 FOUR-CHEESE BURGER 42
GARLIC BUTTER BURGER 45 GREEK BURGER 46 LOUISIANA BURGER 48
MIAMI BURGER 51 NAPA VALLEY BURGER 52 NACHO BURGER 53
OAXACAN BURGER 55 PATTY MELT BURGER 57 PHILADELPHIA BURGER 60
SANTA FE BURGER 63 TRATTORIA BURGER 65
WILD MUSHROOM-CHEDDAR BURGER 66 TURKEY COBB BURGER 69
BLUE BURGER 70 SALMON BURGER WITH HOISIN BARBECUE SAUCE AND
PICKLED GINGER AND NAPA SLAW 71
SALMON BURGER WITH HONEY MUSTARD-DILL SAUCE 74
TUNA BURGER WITH PINEAPPLE-MUSTARD GLAZE AND GREEN
CHILE-PICKLE RELISH 75
PROVENÇAL TUNA BURGER WITH ROASTED GARLIC-TOMATO AIOLI 78

# BURGER ESSENTIALS

**TO ME, THE BURGER IS THE PERFECT SANDWICH, THE PERFECT MEAL, ONE THAT SHOULD NEVER FAIL TO SATISFY. BUT THE HAMBURGER IS TOO OFTEN OVER-LOOKED AND TAKEN FOR GRANTED. SURE, THE BURGER IS INCREDIBLY POPULAR, BUT IS IT TRULY APPRECIATED? A GREAT ONE SHOULD BE. TO ACHIEVE THE BEST BURGER POSSIBLE—AS WITH EVERY SANDWICH—YOU'VE GOT TO TREAT EACH COMPONENT WITH THE THOUGHTFULNESS AND RESPECT IT DESERVES.**

I love a good old-fashioned cheeseburger made with American cheese and topped with some combination of sliced beefsteak tomatoes, dill pickles, raw or grilled sweet onions, ketchup, and spicy horseradish-Dijon mustard. And while that is a classic for good reason, there are some times when I feel like getting a little more creative with my burger. Once I get started, I pull out all the stops in terms of condiments and toppings. I like to be adventurous with my food, and the burger is no exception. So from coleslaw to sautéed mushrooms, from avocado relish to pickled onions, from blue cheese sauce to blue corn tortilla chips, I'm up for it. But don't take that to mean that I am reckless. I put a lot of thought into my burgers and want to make sure that each condiment and topping complements the other and that everything ultimately comes together to make the most delicious burger possible.

I might take a walk on the wild side when it comes to the toppings for my burgers, but I am much more of a purist when it comes to the patty itself. My personal preference is for beef burgers. I do occasionally like a turkey or a fish burger and I appreciate that others do, too, so I have included recipes for such here. But my perfect burger is made with ground beef. You can grind your beef at home, but this is rather time-consuming. I recommend either finding a good butcher who will grind your beef to order or going to a reputable source where beef is ground fresh daily. I try to stay away from prepackaged or preformed patties because I find them to be inconsistent in freshness, texture, and flavor.

My cut of choice for burgers is **ground chuck,** preferably Certified Angus. Chuck is not a pricy cut by any means, but a higher cost doesn't automatically lead to a better end

11

result. I like chuck because of its relatively high fat content: when you look for it in your market, check to see that it is listed as 80 percent lean, 20 percent fat. There is one thing you can't deny: fat carries flavor and moisture. So if you want a juicy, flavorful burger, chuck is definitely the way to go.

This principle applies to **ground turkey,** too. The all-white meat, 99 percent lean ground turkey may look appealing, but I recommend choosing ground turkey with a higher fat content (usually marked as 85 to 90 percent lean). This is a combination of white breast meat and dark meat from the legs and thighs. To my mind, the moist, deeper-flavored dark meat is where it's at, so the more in the mix, the better. You can even get all-dark-meat ground turkey, which is fantastic.

I season my burgers with **kosher salt and freshly ground black** pepper and that's it. Although I will occasionally crust the exterior of a burger with a spice rub (as on the Dallas Burger, page 37), I never mix any spices, herbs, or condiments into the meat itself. Nor do I add ingredients such as onions or garlic or fillers such as eggs or bread crumbs. My reasoning for this is pretty simple: do all of that and you'll have meatloaf. And if you wanted

meatloaf, well then you should just go make that instead. What I'm talking about here is a burger, pure and simple. I do, however, make an exception to my rule when making **fish burgers,** such as salmon or tuna. On the whole, seafood contains very little fat, which is a good thing. But this leanness does mean that fish burgers could use a boost in flavor and moisture. Additional ingredients also help to bind delicate fish into a burger that will hold its shape during cooking.

When forming your burgers, try to mold the meat into uniform, fairly flat patties that are no more than ¾ inch thick. Don't overwork, squeeze, or compress the meat as you shape it or you run the risk of ending up with dry, tough burgers. (If you are making a fish burger, put the patties into the refrigerator at this point and chill for at least 30 minutes. This step helps enable the delicate fish to bind with the other ingredients and form a cohesive burger that will keep its shape when cooked.) Once the patties are shaped, make a deep depression in the center of each burger with your thumb. This does two things. One, it prevents flying saucer–shaped burgers—you know the ones I am talking about: all puffed up and bulging in the center. What's the first

thing you want to do when you see one of those? Press it down with a spatula as it cooks. And what happens when you do that? All the juices run out and you end up with a compacted, dry hockey puck. So, two, making the indentation in the patties helps keep your reflexes in check and ensures juicy, moist burgers. As the meat cooks and expands, the depression magically disappears, leaving you with beautifully shaped and cooked burgers.

Again, I know it's tempting, but you really don't want to press down on your patties as they cook. Not only does pressing squeeze out all of those amazingly flavorful juices, but it can also lead to dangerous flare-ups if you are cooking on a grill, not to mention splattering hot oil all over you and your stovetop if you're cooking inside. While I'm on the topic of safety, there are a couple of things to remember. Ground meat should always be kept in the refrigerator until just before cooking to limit the exposure to airborne bacteria. (My usual advice to let meat sit at room temperature for fifteen minutes before cooking does not carry over to burgers.) Also be sure not to serve or carry cooked meat on the same plate that held it when it was raw, as it may be contaminated with bacteria from the uncooked meat.

You can make the perfect burger just about anywhere, inside or out. Grilling is a great method; the large surface of a grill area makes it especially useful when feeding a crowd. Any sturdy grill will do; just make sure the grill is hot. A **gas grill** should be set to high and the coals of a **charcoal grill** should be heated until they burn bright orange and turn ashy.

My favorite way to cook a burger indoors is on **cast iron**, either in a **skillet** or **grill pan**, or on a **griddle**. Cast iron has excellent heat diffusion and retention properties and produces evenly cooked burgers with a really great crust. Cast-iron pans are inexpensive and with proper care can last a lifetime—or longer. Most cast-iron pans can be purchased preseasoned, or you can season it yourself before use. The majority of cast-iron pans on the market today, including those in my line for Kohl's (see Resources, page 156), come preseasoned. These will occasionally need to be reseasoned, and you do this in the same way that you would prepare an unseasoned pan before use. It's a very simply process: coat your pan inside and out with a thin layer of vegetable oil and place it upside down on the top rack of a 350- to 400-degree-F oven for an hour. After an hour, turn the oven off and allow the pan to cool completely in the oven. Once it is cool, you are ready to go!

A **stainless-steel sauté pan or skillet** is an all-around good choice for cooking just about anything, including burgers. Most have an aluminum core, which helps to distribute and retain heat; if you are in the market for a new stainless-steel pan, make sure that it has this aluminum core.

**Nonstick pans** are the best choice for cooking fish burgers because fish is quite delicate and the burgers have a tendency to fall apart on or stick to other surfaces. I do not like to make beef or turkey burgers in nonstick pans, however, because they do not develop the tasty crust that they would on a grill or other type of pan.

We've got the burger covered; now we just need something to put it on. My perfect **bun** has to be soft, either with or without sesame seeds. I am not overly fond of the trend of serving burgers on artisanal breads because I usually find them to be too hard. They also tend to break up the burger when you bite into it and can turn eating your burger into a fork and knife endeavor. (And burgers should never, ever be a fork and knife endeavor.) The way I see it, a burger is a sandwich and is meant to be eaten as such—with your hands. A soft bun makes that possible by almost molding itself around its contents.

Just because your bun is soft does not mean that it has to be tasteless. Softness and flavor are not mutually exclusive, so do what you can to find a good-quality soft bun. I want it soft, yes, but not airy, and it should have enough body not to disintegrate under a juicy burger. As far as supermarket offerings are concerned, look for a bun made by a brand whose sandwich bread you know and trust. I usually go with Pepperidge Farm sesame seeded hamburger buns. I also recommend trying potato bread hamburger buns. They are tender yet substantial with an appealing touch of sweetness.

I think the taste and the texture of buns are best when lightly toasted. To toast a bun on a grill, grill pan, or griddle, split the bun open, place it cut side down on the grill, and grill until light golden brown, about 10 seconds. Alternatively, you can place the split bun halves cut side up on a baking sheet and cook them under a preheated broiler until light golden brown, about 30 seconds. Keep a close eye on them and don't let them get too brown or else that texture will take on a life of its own and defeat the purpose of starting with a soft bun.

# PERFECT BURGER

**SERVES 4**

> 1½ pounds ground chuck (80 percent lean)
>   or ground turkey (90 percent lean)
> Kosher salt and freshly ground
>   black pepper
> 1½ tablespoons canola oil
> 4 slices cheese (optional)
> 4 hamburger buns, split; toasted
>   (see page 15), if desired

**1.** Divide the meat into 4 equal portions (about 6 ounces each). Form each portion loosely into a ¾-inch-thick burger and make a deep depression in the center with your thumb. Season both sides of each burger with salt and pepper.

**2.** IF USING A GRILL: Heat a gas grill to high or heat coals in a charcoal grill until they glow bright orange and ash over. Brush the burgers with the oil. Grill the burgers until golden brown and slightly charred on the first side, about 3 minutes for beef and 5 minutes for turkey. Flip over the burgers. Cook beef burgers until golden brown and slightly charred on the second side, 4 minutes for medium rare (3 minutes if topping with cheese; see step 3) or until cooked to desired degree of doneness (see page 17 for approximate cooking times). Cook turkey burgers until cooked throughout, about 5 minutes on the second side.

IF USING A GRILL PAN: Heat a grill pan over high heat on top of the stove. Cook the burgers as for a grill, above.

IF USING A SAUTÉ PAN OR GRIDDLE (PREFER-ABLY CAST IRON): Heat the oil in the pan or griddle over high heat until the oil begins to shimmer. Cook the burgers until golden brown and slightly charred on the first side, about 3 minutes for beef and 5 minutes for turkey. Flip over the burgers. Cook beef burgers until golden brown and slightly charred on the second side, 4 minutes for medium rare (3 minutes if topping with cheese; see step 3) or until cooked to desired degree of doneness (see page 17 for approximate cooking times). Cook turkey burgers until cooked throughout, about 5 minutes on the second side.

**3.** Add the cheese, if using, to the tops of the burgers during the last minute of cooking and top with a basting cover (see page 21), close the grill cover, or tent the burgers with aluminum foil to melt the cheese.

**4.** Sandwich the hot burgers between the buns and serve immediately.

# COOKING TIMES FOR BURGERS

To me, a perfect **beef burger** is pink and juicy in the middle and cooked some-
where between medium-rare and medium, which is an internal temperature of
about 145 degrees F. The USDA recommends cooking ground beef until it
reaches an internal temperature of 160 degrees F for safety reasons. Burgers
destined for those who are very young or very old, pregnant, or have compro-
mised immune systems should definitely be cooked until well done.

**Rare:** approximately 6 minutes total cooking time
**Medium-rare:** approximately 7 minutes total cooking time
**Medium:** approximately 8 minutes total cooking time
**Medium-well:** approximately 9 minutes total cooking time
**Well:** approximately 10 minutes total cooking time
**Well done:** approximately 11 minutes total cooking time

**Turkey burgers** and **chicken burgers,** for that matter, must be cooked
completely through to prevent salmonella poisoning. But since the bacteria is killed
at 165 degrees F, you can cook your burgers to medium-well doneness, which is
an approximate internal temperature of 165 degrees F.

PROVOLONE

MOZZARELLA

GRUYÈRE

CHEDDAR

FETA

BLUE

QUESO FRESCO

AMERICAN

MONTEREY JACK

# CHEESEBURGER ESSENTIALS

**I UNDERSTAND THAT THERE IS A CONTINGENT OF PEOPLE OUT THERE WHO DON'T CARE FOR CHEESE ON THEIR BURGERS. I SUPPOSE I CAN UNDERSTAND WANTING TO SAVOR THE TASTE OF PURE BEEF WITHOUT ANY INTERFERENCE FROM CHEESE . . . MAYBE. PERSONALLY, I AM A CHEESEBURGER FANATIC. I WANT CHEESE ON MY BURGER AND LOTS OF IT. I AM ALMOST ALWAYS GAME FOR A CHEESEBURGER MADE WITH AMERICAN CHEESE—I JUST LOVE HOW IT MELTS—BUT THERE ARE OTHER CHEESES THAT CAN BRING A LOT MORE FLAVOR TO YOUR BURGER. HERE IS A LIST OF THE CHEESES THAT I CALL FOR IN THIS BOOK.**

## AMERICAN

This is the cheese that most of us grew up on, at least for our cheeseburgers. It is a mild-tasting processed cheese with a medium-firm consistency and a great melting ability. It comes in both yellow and white varieties but the difference is only aesthetic. I dislike the individually wrapped slices and recommend getting it sliced from the deli. I know that American cheese gets a bad rap, but I think it is great on cheeseburgers because it melts so well and fuses the burger to the bun.

## BLUE

Sharp and tangy, blue cheese can be made from cow's, sheep's, or goat's milk and is generally ivory in color and shot through with varying concentrations of blue or blue-green veins. Blue cheese melts beautifully into sauces and is wonderful crumbled on top of a burger. There are many varieties of blue cheese out there, from the Italian Gorgonzola to the French Roquefort. My personal favorites are American Maytag and Spanish Cabrales, but you should pick a favorite from what is available to you.

## CHEDDAR

Cheddar is the most widely purchased and eaten cheese in the world. It originated in England but is now made all over the world. In this country,

Wisconsin, New York, and Vermont are all known for their excellent cheddar cheese. Always made from cow's milk, cheddar ranges from smooth when young to slightly crumbly when aged. While good-quality cheddar will bring great flavor to your burger, it doesn't melt particularly well and can get a bit oily when heated. I still like it; it's just not my all-time favorite.

## FETA

Feta cheese is traditionally made in Greece with sheep's or goat's milk, but you will also find French, Bulgarian, and American varieties, including some made with cow's milk. Cakes of white feta are salted and cured in a brine solution. Salty and tangy, feta can range from mild to sharp in flavor and from soft to semi-hard in texture. Feta will soften slightly when heated on a burger but it doesn't really melt. What it does do is add loads of salty, briny flavor.

## FONTINA

Fontina is an Italian cow's milk cheese. (There are also Danish and domestic derivatives, but the Italian is the original.) This semi-firm, creamy cheese is dotted with small irregular holes and is pale yellow in color with a golden brown or reddish rind. It is mild, nutty, and melts incredibly well.

### GRUYÈRE/SWISS
Gruyère is a sweet yet slightly salty hard yellow cow's milk cheese named after Gruyère, Switzerland. Its flavor and texture are greatly dependent upon its age, starting out as creamy and nutty and getting progressively more assertive, earthy, and complex as it ages. The fuller aged Gruyère will develop small holes and cracks and have a slightly grainy texture. If you can't find Gruyère, use Swiss cheese in its place.

### MANCHEGO
Manchego is perhaps the definitive cheese of Spain. Made from sheep's milk, it is piquant, buttery, and nutty. Manchego is available in two varieties: *curado* (cured), which is aged 3 to 4 months and has a semi-soft texture ideal for melting, and *viejo* (aged), which is more intensely flavored and has a firmer texture akin to that of Parmesan.

### MONTEREY JACK
Monterey Jack is an American semi-hard cheese, originally from Northern California, made from cow's milk. It has a mild taste. Most of the Monterey Jack cheese that you will find is aged for a short time (about a month), is rather soft, and is great for melting.

### MOZZARELLA
There are two kinds of mozzarella: the low-moisture version, which is sold in plastic-sealed bricks or shredded in bags in the refrigerated section of your grocery, and the fresh version, which has a high moisture content and is either served the day it is made or packed in brine. Low-moisture mozzarella is firmer and more ivory in color than fresh. Both are mild in taste and melt well, though the fresh will not spread quite as much as the packaged. Even so, I prefer the clean flavor of fresh mozzarella.

### PROVOLONE
Provolone is a semi-hard, whole-milk cow's cheese that originated in Italy and is therefore a great cheese to pair with other Italian-influenced burger toppings. Provolone is aged for a minimum of four months and has a slightly sharp taste.

### QUESO FRESCO
Queso fresco is a Mexican cow's milk cheese whose name literally translates as "fresh cheese." It is a firm white cheese with a slightly salty, mild, yet tangy taste, somewhat akin to that of farmer's cheese. It crumbles much like feta and is normally used on dishes like enchiladas and tamales and as a garnish for black bean and tortilla soups. It will not melt but it does become soft when heated.

Now that you know what kind of cheese you're going to use, we have to talk about how to melt it. There is nothing I hate more than getting a cheeseburger with cheese that hasn't been melted all the way. Now, I'm not talking about feta or something that doesn't really melt all that well in the first place. But it's a crying shame when the mozzarella on top of your burger isn't oozing down the sides and making a delicious mess when you bite into it.

Getting the perfect melt is so easy to accomplish. Here's my secret: I use a **basting cover,** an inexpensive aluminum dome that short-order cooks use in diners. It looks like the lid of a sauté pan, except that it is domed to fit over the burger. A basting cover allows just enough clearance, meaning the cheese doesn't touch and stick to it but the cover can still hold in the heat to melt the cheese beautifully. If you don't have a basting cover, a sturdy metal bowl will also do the trick. Alternatively, you can close the grill cover or you can even tent each burger with a square of aluminum foil.

# ARGENTINEAN BURGER

Argentineans are well-known for their beef and for their love of the grill. Just about everything that comes off of the Argentinean grill is garnished with chimichurri, a bright herbaceous mixture of fresh parsley, garlic, red wine vinegar, and olive oil. It could very well be the national condiment. Knowing what an affinity grilled meats and chimichurri have for one another, it makes sense that a burger would benefit from a dose of vibrant chimichurri as well. Rings of deep red onion and slices of slightly salty Manchego cheese finish the burger to perfection.

**SERVES 4**

## CHIMICHURRI

2 cups packed fresh flat-leaf parsley leaves
1 tablespoon fresh oregano leaves
4 cloves garlic
1 teaspoon smoked sweet Spanish paprika
3 tablespoons red wine vinegar
½ cup extra-virgin olive oil
Kosher salt and freshly ground
    black pepper

## BURGERS

1½ pounds ground chuck (80 percent lean)
    or ground turkey (90 percent lean)
Kosher salt and freshly ground
    black pepper
1½ tablespoons canola oil
4 slices Manchego cheese
4 hamburger buns, split; toasted
    (see page 15), if desired
½ red onion, sliced ¼ inch thick

**1.** To make the chimichurri, combine the parsley, oregano, and garlic in a food processor and pulse until coarsely chopped. Add the paprika, vinegar, and oil, season with salt and pepper, and process until smooth. Scrape into a bowl. Let sit at room temperature for 30 minutes before serving. The sauce can be made 8 hours in advance, tightly covered, and refrigerated. Bring to room temperature before serving.

**2.** Divide the meat into 4 equal portions (about 6 ounces each). Form each portion loosely into a ¾-inch-thick burger and make a deep depression in the center with your thumb. Season both sides of each burger with salt and pepper.

**3.** Cook the burgers, using the oil (see page 16) and topping each one with a slice of cheese and a basting cover during the last minute of cooking (see page 2).

**4.** Place the burgers on the bun bottoms and top with a large dollop of the sauce and sliced onion. Cover with the bun tops and serve immediately.

# ARTHUR AVENUE BURGER

In a city full of Italian restaurants and specialty shops, Arthur Avenue in the Bronx is where you'll find New York City's most authentic Southern Italian fare. With its generations-old mom-and-pop businesses, this area of town seems as though it is stuck in a time warp—and I mean that in the most positive way possible. Arthur Avenue is the place to go when you want the real deal, from great eggplant Parmesan to baked ziti to mouthwatering Italian sandwiches. This burger, with its crispy frico made from nutty Fontina cheese, and a garlic- and chile-infused ketchup, is my ode to that famous neighborhood.

**SERVES 4**

### FRA DIAVOLO KETCHUP
1 tablespoon olive oil
3 cloves garlic, finely chopped
¼ teaspoon red chile flakes
¾ cup ketchup
2 teaspoons finely chopped fresh oregano leaves
2 teaspoons red wine vinegar
2 tablespoons finely chopped fresh basil leaves
Kosher salt and freshly ground black pepper

### FONTINA FRICOS
¾ cup grated Fontina cheese
2 teaspoons all-purpose flour

### BURGERS
1½ pounds ground chuck (80 percent lean) or ground turkey (90 percent lean)
Kosher salt and freshly ground black pepper
1½ tablespoons canola oil

4 ciabatta rolls or sesame seed hamburger buns, split; toasted (see page 15), if desired
1 handful of baby arugula leaves

**1.** To make the ketchup, heat the oil in a small nonreactive saucepan over medium heat. Add the garlic and chile flakes and cook for 1 minute. Add the ketchup and oregano and cook for 2 minutes. Remove from the heat and stir in the vinegar and basil and season with salt and pepper. Transfer to a bowl and let cool to room temperature or cover and refrigerate for up to 1 day. Bring to room temperature before serving.

**2.** To make the fricos, combine the cheese and flour in a bowl. Heat an 8-inch nonstick pan over medium-high heat. Add 3 tablespoons of the cheese mixture and cook until light brown on the bottom. Turn over with a heat-proof silicone spatula and continue cooking for another 10 to 15 seconds. Remove to a plate to cool. Wipe out the pan with a paper towel and repeat to make 3 more fricos.

**3.** Divide the meat into 4 equal portions (about 6 ounces each). Form each portion loosely into a ¾-inch-thick burger and make a deep depression in the center with your thumb. Season both sides of each burger with salt and pepper. Cook the burgers, using the oil (see page 16).

**4.** Place the burgers on the bun bottoms. Add some of the arugula to each burger, top with the fricos, and then add a dollop of the ketchup. Top with the bun tops and serve immediately.

# BISTRO BURGER

One of my favorite bistro meals consists of a thick and juicy steak crusted with coarsely ground black pepper–steak au poivre–served with a simple green salad tossed with a mustardy vinaigrette. The bistro burger takes the flavor highlights of that meal and packages them in burger form. The coarse black pepper makes a great crust for the burger –just as it does on steak au poivre!—and adds a nice touch of heat. Shredded endive in a mustard vinaigrette (of course) and nutty Gruyère cheese are natural accompaniments.

**SERVES 4**

3 tablespoons white wine vinegar
1 heaping tablespoon Dijon mustard
Kosher salt and freshly ground
    black pepper
⅓ cup extra-virgin olive oil
1 large head of endive, thinly shredded
1½ pounds ground chuck (80 percent lean)
    or ground turkey (90 percent lean)
1 teaspoon coarsely ground black pepper
1½ tablespoons canola oil
4 slices Gruyère cheese, each ¼ inch thick
4 brioche or regular hamburger buns, split;
    toasted (see page 15), if desired

**1.** Whisk together the vinegar and mustard in a medium bowl and season with salt and pepper. Slowly add the olive oil and whisk until emulsified. Add the endive to the bowl and toss to coat. Let sit at room temperature for 15 minutes before serving.

**2.** Divide the meat into 4 equal portions (about 6 ounces each). Form each portion loosely into a ¾-inch-thick burger and make a deep depression in the center with your thumb. Season both sides of each burger with salt and with the coarsely ground black pepper.

**3.** Cook the burgers, using the oil (see page 16) and topping each one with a slice of cheese and a basting cover during the last minute of cooking (see page 21).

**4.** Place the burgers on the bun bottoms and top each one with some of the endive. Cover with the bun tops and serve immediately.

# BUFFALO BURGER

I'm not talking about bison here; I'm talking about the sauce that made Buffalo, New York, famous. I took two of my favorite football-watching foods and melded them into one. Buffalo wing, meet the burger! Hot sauce and tangy blue cheese have found a new home. For an appetizer, make bite-size sliders if you want. Another way to go would be to make this burger with ground turkey or . . . that's right, ground chicken.

**SERVES 4**

1½ pounds ground chuck (80 percent lean)
    or ground turkey (90 percent lean)
Kosher salt and freshly ground
    black pepper
1½ tablespoons canola oil
½ cup hot sauce
4 sesame seed hamburger buns, split;
    toasted (see page 15), if desired
Blue Cheese Sauce (page 110) or 2 ounces
    blue cheese, crumbled (about ½ cup)

**1.** Divide the meat into 4 equal portions (about 6 ounces each). Form each portion loosely into a ¾-inch-thick burger and make a deep depression in the center with your thumb. Season both sides of each burger with salt and pepper. Cook the burgers, using the oil (see page 16).

**2.** Brush the burgers with some of the hot sauce, flip over onto a plate, and brush the other sides of the burgers with more of the hot sauce. Place the burgers on the bun bottoms and slather with some of the blue cheese sauce. Cover with the bun tops and serve immediately.

# BOLO BURGER

This burger proved itself eternally popular on the lunchtime menu of my Spanish-inspired restaurant, Bolo. It is definitely an upscale burger, featuring premium Spanish ingredients such as Serrano ham, Manchego cheese, and piquillo peppers. The rich and smoky aioli comes together in a flash but you'd never know that from its complex, spicy-sweet taste. Pressing the whole thing gives the bun a nice crispness and also marries all of the elements into a cohesive dish.

**SERVES 4**

### PIQUILLO PEPPER–SMOKED PAPRIKA AIOLI

½ cup mayonnaise
2 cloves garlic, chopped
2 jarred piquillo peppers, drained
2 teaspoons smoked sweet Spanish paprika
½ teaspoon kosher salt

### BURGERS

1½ pounds ground chuck (80 percent lean) or ground turkey (90 percent lean)
Kosher salt and freshly ground black pepper
3 tablespoons canola oil
4 sesame seed hamburger buns, split; toasted (see page 15), if desired
8 slices Manchego cheese
8 paper-thin slices Serrano ham

**1.** To make the aioli, combine the mayonnaise, garlic, peppers, paprika, and salt in a food processor and process until smooth. Cover and refrigerate for at least 30 minutes before serving. The aioli can be prepared 1 day in advance, tightly covered, and refrigerated.

**2.** Divide the meat into 4 equal portions (about 6 ounces each). Form each portion loosely into a ¾-inch-thick burger and make a deep depression in the center with your thumb. Season both sides of each burger with salt and pepper. Cook the burgers, using 1½ tablespoons of the oil (see page 16).

**3.** Place the bun bottoms on a flat surface and spread half of the aioli over them. Top each one with a slice of cheese, then a slice of the ham, then a burger, another slice of ham, and finally another slice of cheese, in that order. Spread the rest of the aioli on the bun tops and cover each burger with a top.

**4.** Brush the tops of the buns with the remaining 1½ tablespoons of oil and place on the grill, griddle, or sauté pan, top side down. Using a heavy-duty metal spatula, press down on the bottom of the buns and grill until the tops are light golden brown, 1 to 2 minutes. Turn the burgers over and continue cooking, pressing down on the tops, until the bottoms are light golden brown and the cheese has melted, about 1 minute longer. Serve immediately.

# BREAKFAST BURGER

There are some mornings—and they usually come after a long night—when all I can think about is a breakfast sandwich piled high with eggs, bacon, and cheese. Add a side of hash browns and I might as well be in heaven. Given my love of a good breakfast sandwich, it was only a matter of time before I decided to move that sandwich out of breakfast-only terrain and into a burger. Breakfast, lunch, dinner . . . now I can get my fix any time. I prefer my egg cooked over easy because I love how the yolk runs out and saturates the burger after the first bite, but if that's not your thing, you should of course cook the eggs according to your preference.

SERVES 4

1½ pounds ground chuck (80 percent lean) or ground turkey (90 percent lean)
Kosher salt and freshly ground black pepper
1½ tablespoons canola oil, or more, if needed
4 slices American cheese (optional)
4 large eggs
4 hamburger buns, split; toasted (see page 15), if desired
8 slices crisp cooked bacon
½ recipe Shoestring Fries (page 98)
Chipotle Ketchup (page 112; optional)

**1.** Divide the meat into 4 equal portions (about 6 ounces each). Form each portion loosely into a ¾-inch-thick burger and make a deep depression in the center with your thumb. Season both sides of each burger with salt and pepper.

**2.** Cook the burgers, using the 2 tablespoons oil (see page 16) and topping each one with a slice of cheese and a basting cover during the last minute of cooking (see page 21). Remove the burgers to a plate and loosely tent with aluminum foil.

**3.** If you used a griddle or sauté pan to cook the burgers, reduce the heat under it to medium. If you used a grill, heat a tablespoon or two of oil in a medium sauté pan over medium heat. Crack the eggs into the pan and season with salt and pepper. Let the eggs cook until the whites just set up, about 45 seconds. Gently flip the eggs over (trying not to break the yolks) and cook for 10 seconds.

**4.** Place the burgers on the bun bottoms and top with the bacon and some of the shoestring fries. Drizzle the fries with chipotle ketchup and place the eggs on top of the fries. Top with the bun tops and serve immediately.

# CAESAR SALAD BURGER

The classically American Caesar salad has taken on a life of its own. Forget about it as a starter—this salad has become a meal on menus across the country with the addition of chicken, steak, or shrimp. Why not take it one step further and put the salad on a burger? Refreshing romaine lettuce lends its crispness to the burger, but the zesty dressing and extra Parmesan cheese are what really make this so identifiable flavor-wise and so tasty. All of the classic components of Caesar dressing—garlic, Worcestershire sauce, anchovies (these can be your secret, but their rich saltiness is essential)—morph into a slightly spicy mayonnaise perfect for spreading all over this new way to make a meal out of Caesar salad.

**SERVES 4**

### CAESAR MAYONNAISE
½ cup mayonnaise
1 tablespoon Dijon mustard
2 cloves garlic, chopped
2 anchovy fillets
1 tablespoon fresh lemon juice
2 dashes Tabasco sauce
2 dashes Worcestershire sauce
¼ teaspoon freshly ground black pepper
2 tablespoons freshly grated
    Parmesan cheese, plus more for garnish

### BURGERS
1½ pounds ground chuck (80 percent lean)
    or ground turkey (90 percent lean)
Kosher salt and freshly ground
    black pepper
1½ tablespoons canola oil
4 hamburger buns, split; toasted
    (see page 15), if desired
12 romaine heart leaves
2 tablespoons freshly grated
    Parmesan cheese

**1.** To make the Caesar mayonnaise, combine the mayonnaise, mustard, garlic, anchovies, lemon juice, Tabasco, Worcestershire sauce, and pepper in a food processor and process until smooth. Scrape into a bowl and stir in the cheese. Cover and refrigerate for at least 30 minutes or up to 8 hours before serving to allow the flavors to meld.

**2.** Divide the meat into 4 equal portions (about 6 ounces each). Form each portion loosely into a ¾-inch-thick burger and make a deep depression in the center with your thumb. Season both sides of each burger with salt and pepper. Cook the burgers, using the oil (see page 16).

**3.** Place the burgers on the bun bottoms and spread a few tablespoons of the Caesar mayonnaise on each burger. Top with the romaine leaves and sprinkle with Parmesan and black pepper. Cover with the bun tops and serve immediately.

# CALIFORNIA BURGER

From fruit to dairy, the farms of California yield so many fantastic ingredients. Two of my favorites are pebbly-skinned Hass avocados and Monterey Jack cheese. In fact, the two are somewhat similar in their mild taste and creamy consistency. To create a bit more contrast in flavor and texture, I nix simply sliced avocados in favor of a chunky avocado relish made with diced onion, bright leaves of cilantro, fresh lime juice, and a touch of spicy jalapeño.

SERVES 4

### AVOCADO RELISH

2 ripe Hass avocados, halved, pitted, peeled, and coarsely chopped
½ small onion, finely diced
1 jalapeño chile, finely diced
Juice of 1 lime
¼ cup finely chopped fresh cilantro leaves
Kosher salt and freshly ground black pepper

### BURGERS

1½ pounds ground chuck (80 percent lean) or ground turkey (90 percent lean)
Kosher salt and freshly ground black pepper
1½ tablespoons canola oil
4 slices Monterey Jack cheese
4 hamburger buns, split; toasted (see page 15), if desired
1 small bunch of watercress
4 slices ripe beefsteak tomato

**1.** To make the avocado relish, combine the avocados, onion, jalapeño, lime juice, and cilantro in a small bowl and season with salt and pepper. The relish can be made up to 1 hour in advance and kept at room temperature.

**2.** Divide the meat into 4 equal portions (about 6 ounces each). Form each portion loosely into a ¾-inch-thick burger and make a deep depression in the center with your thumb. Season both sides of each burger with salt and pepper.

**3.** Cook the burgers, using the oil (see page 16) and topping each one with a slice of cheese and a basting cover during the last minute of cooking (see page 21).

**4.** Place the burgers on the bun bottoms and top each one with a few sprigs of watercress, a slice of tomato, and a dollop of the avocado relish. Cover with the bun tops and serve immediately.

# CAROLINA BURGER

Just mention the Carolinas and I immediately think of pulled pork sandwiches, dripping with barbecue sauce and topped with creamy coleslaw. Take the pulled pork out of the equation, add the rest to a burger, and you've got the Carolina Burger. It's all about finding a great home for those sweet, vinegary, and spicy flavors that go so well with coleslaw.

**SERVES 4**

### MUSTARD BARBECUE SAUCE

¼ cup rice wine vinegar
2 heaping tablespoons Dijon mustard
2 tablespoons honey
1 teaspoon kosher salt
¼ cup extra-virgin olive oil
¾ teaspoon coarsely ground black pepper

### GREEN ONION SLAW

1 cup coarsely chopped green onions, white and green parts
¼ cup red wine vinegar
2 serrano chiles, stemmed and seeded
2 tablespoons mayonnaise
¼ cup olive oil
Kosher salt and freshly ground black pepper
½ head of purple cabbage, finely shredded (about 3 cups)
1 small red onion, halved and thinly sliced
¼ cup chopped fresh cilantro leaves

### BURGERS

1½ pounds ground chuck (80 percent lean) or ground turkey (90 percent lean)
Kosher salt and freshly ground black pepper

1½ tablespoons canola oil
4 hamburger buns, split; toasted (see page 15), if desired

**1.** To make the mustard barbecue sauce, blend the vinegar, mustard, honey, salt, and oil in a blender until emulsified. Transfer to a bowl and stir in the black pepper. The barbecue sauce can be made 1 day ahead, covered, and refrigerated. Bring to room temperature before serving.

**2.** To make the dressing for the slaw, blend the green onions, vinegar, ¼ cup cold water, chiles, mayonnaise, and oil in a blender until emulsified. Season with salt and pepper. Put the cabbage and red onion in a bowl, add the dressing, and stir until combined. Fold in the cilantro and season with salt and pepper to taste. Let sit at room temperature for at least 15 minutes before serving. The slaw can be made 2 hours in advance and refrigerated.

**3.** Divide the meat into 4 equal portions (about 6 ounces each). Form each portion loosely into a ¾-inch-thick burger and make a deep depression in the center with your thumb. Season both sides of each burger with salt and pepper. Cook the burgers, using the oil (see page 16), and basting the burgers with some of the barbecue sauce during the last minute of cooking.

**4.** Place the burgers on the bun bottoms and top each one with more barbecue sauce and some of the slaw. Cover with the bun tops and serve immediately.

# DALLAS BURGER

I have to tip my hat to my wife for this one. She is a Texas girl through and through, and she loves her beef brisket with coleslaw and pickles. I do, too, but I don't necessarily have the patience to wait for the brisket. This burger satisfies her craving for a taste of home and my need for speed, all in one, making it a classic in our house. This burger has even proved popular with the patrons of Bobby's Burger Palace.

**SERVES 4**

### COLESLAW
¾ cup mayonnaise
½ small white onion, grated
1 tablespoon sugar
2 teaspoons celery seed
3 tablespoons apple cider vinegar
1 small head of cabbage, cored
   and finely shredded
1 large carrot, finely shredded
Kosher salt and freshly ground black
   pepper

### BURGERS
1 tablespoon ancho chile powder
2 teaspoons sweet Spanish paprika
1 teaspoon dry mustard powder
1 teaspoon ground cumin
1 teaspoon ground coriander
1 teaspoon dried oregano
1 teaspoon kosher salt
½ teaspoon freshly ground black pepper
½ teaspoon chile de árbol powder
   or cayenne pepper

1½ pounds ground chuck (80 percent lean)
   or ground turkey (90 percent lean)
1½ tablespoons canola oil
Barbecue Sauce (page 107)
4 hamburger buns, split; toasted
   (see page 15), if desired
Homemade Dill Pickles (page 113)

**1.** To make the coleslaw, whisk together the mayonnaise, onion, sugar, celery seed, and vinegar in a large bowl. Add the cabbage and carrot, season with salt and pepper, and stir to combine. Let sit for at least 15 minutes and up to 1 hour before serving.

**2.** To make the burgers, whisk together the ancho powder, paprika, dried mustard powder, cumin, coriander, oregano, salt, black pepper, and chile de árbol powder in a small bowl.

**3.** Divide the meat into 4 equal portions (about 6 ounces each). Form each portion loosely into a ¾-inch-thick burger and make a deep depression in the center with your thumb. Season both sides of each burger with the spice mixture.

**4.** Cook the burgers, using the canola oil (see page 16) and brushing with some of the barbecue sauce after you flip them.

**5.** Place the burgers on the bun bottoms and spoon more barbecue sauce on top. Top each one with some of the coleslaw and a few pickles. Cover with the bun tops and serve immediately.

# CHEYENNE BURGER

I admit it, my roots are just about as city slicker as they come. Still, there's a part of me that identifies with the cowboy mentality of the West. I once went to a rodeo in Cheyenne, Wyoming, and one of the things that I took away from that experience was the idea for this burger; it just seems like perfect rodeo fare. While in my mind's eye the Cheyenne burger is best devoured at that rodeo or maybe while sitting around a campfire, I think its layers of smoked cheddar, spicy barbecue sauce, and crispy fried onions would bring out the cowboy in anyone, anywhere. Feeling extra adventurous? Add a couple slices of crisp bacon to the mix.

**SERVES 4**

1½ pounds ground chuck (80 percent lean)
    or ground turkey (90 percent lean)
Kosher salt and freshly ground
    black pepper
1½ tablespoons canola oil
8 slices smoked sharp cheddar
    cheese
4 hamburger buns, split; toasted
    (see page 15), if desired
½ cup Barbecue Sauce (page 107)
8 slices crisp cooked bacon (optional)
½ recipe Shoestring Onion Rings
    (page 101)
Chopped fresh flat-leaf parsley leaves,
    for garnish

**1.** Divide the meat into 4 equal portions (about 6 ounces each). Form each portion loosely into a ¾-inch-thick burger and make a deep depression in the center with your thumb. Season both sides of each burger with salt and pepper.

**2.** Cook the burgers, using the oil (see page 16) and topping each one with a slice of cheese and a basting cover during the last minute of cooking (see page 21).

**3.** Place the burgers on the bun bottoms and slather each one with barbecue sauce. Top with bacon, if using, shoestring onion rings, parsley, and then the bun tops and serve immediately.

# CRUNCHBURGER (AKA THE SIGNATURE BURGER)

This is the "house" burger at Bobby's Burger Palace. It's a basic burger (I like it garnished with red onion, tomato, romaine lettuce, and horseradish mustard) with CRUNCH. The crunch factor comes from a big handful of potato chips layered between the burger and the bun. Some of you may have added chips to your sandwiches as kids, and if people ever told you that you were nuts, I'm here to say that you're not! Oozing melted cheese becomes a part of the chips and those crunchy chips become a part of the burger—delicious. I love getting a mouthful of juicy burger and salty, crispy potato chips in one bite; it's a way to get a true contrast of textures into your cheeseburger. In fact, I make it an option to have all of the burgers at Bobby's Burger Palace "crunchified."

SERVES 4

1½ pounds ground chuck (80 percent lean)
    or ground turkey (90 percent lean)
Kosher salt and freshly ground
    black pepper
1½ tablespoons canola oil
8 slices American cheese, each
    ¼ inch thick
4 potato hamburger buns, split; toasted
    (see page 15), if desired
4 slices beefsteak tomato (optional)
4 leaves romaine lettuce (optional)
4 slices red onion (optional)
Horseradish Mustard Mayonnaise
    (page 109), optional
4 handfuls of potato chips

**1.** Divide the meat into 4 equal portions (about 6 ounces each). Form each portion loosely into a ¾-inch-thick burger and make a deep depression in the center with your thumb. Season both sides of each burger with salt and pepper.

**2.** Cook the burgers, using the oil (see page 16) and topping each one with 2 slices of cheese and a basting cover during the last minute of cooking (see page 21).

**3.** Place the burgers on the bun bottoms and, if desired, top with tomato, lettuce, onion, and a dollop of horseradish mustard mayonnaise. Pile on the potato chips, top with the bun tops, and serve immediately.

# FOUR-CHEESE BURGER

Perhaps this should be called Burger *Quattro Formaggi* after the classic Italian pasta dish or just simply the Cheese Lover's Burger. You can use any types of cheese you like; I just happen to like this combination of nutty Swiss, creamy American, tangy goat, and salty Parmesan. All this burger needs is a thick slice of red beefsteak tomato and a few leaves of fresh arugula, a sort of homage to the Italian flag.

SERVES 4

    1½ pounds ground chuck (80 percent lean)
        or ground turkey (90 percent lean)
    Kosher salt and freshly ground
        black pepper
    1½ tablespoons canola oil
    4 slices Swiss cheese
    4 slices ripe beefsteak tomato, each
        1 inch thick
    4 slices American cheese
    4 round slices fresh goat cheese, each
        ½ inch thick
    ¼ cup freshly grated Parmesan cheese
    4 hamburger buns, split; toasted
        (see page 15), if desired
    1 handful of arugula leaves

**1.** Divide the meat into 4 equal portions (about 6 ounces each). Form each portion loosely into a ¾-inch-thick burger and make a deep depression in the center with your thumb. Season both sides of each burger with salt and pepper.

**2.** Cook the burgers, using the oil (see page 16) and topping each one with a slice of Swiss and a basting cover during the last minute of cooking (see page 21). Add the tomato slices to the grill or pan, cover each with a slice of American, a slice of goat, and some Parmesan. Cover and melt for 1 minute.

**3.** Arrange some arugula on the bun bottoms and top each with a burger and a tomato slice. Cover with the bun tops and serve immediately.

# GARLIC BUTTER BURGER

It doesn't get much easier or much better than this. Basting both the burgers as you cook them and the buns before you toast them with a savory garlicky butter adds a whole new dimension of flavor to a classic burger. Try adding a few tablespoons of fresh herbs or a few dashes of Worcestershire sauce to the butter for even more flavor.

SERVES 4

12 tablespoons (1½ sticks) unsalted butter, slightly softened
4 cloves garlic
½ small shallot, chopped
3 tablespoons chopped fresh flat-leaf parsley leaves
Kosher salt and freshly ground black pepper
1½ pounds ground chuck (80 percent lean) or ground turkey (90 percent lean)
1½ tablespoons canola oil
4 hamburger buns, split

**1.** Combine the butter, garlic, shallot, and parsley in a food processor and process until smooth; season with salt and pepper to taste. Scrape into a bowl, cover, and refrigerate for at least 30 minutes to allow the flavors to meld. The butter will keep in the refrigerator for up to 24 hours. Bring to room temperature before using.

**2.** Divide the meat into 4 equal portions (about 6 ounces each). Form each portion loosely into a ¾-inch-thick burger and make a deep depression in the center with your thumb. Season both sides of each burger with salt and pepper.

**3.** Brush the buns with about 4 tablespoons of the butter, using roughly ½ tablespoon for each half.

**4.** Cook the burgers, using the oil (see page 16) and brushing them every 30 seconds with the remaining garlic butter.

**5.** Meanwhile, toast the buns (see page 15). Place the burgers on the bun bottoms, cover with the bun tops, and serve immediately.

# GREEK BURGER

I have always loved Greek food, and a trip to Greece a few summers ago only reinforced that affection. The Greeks are doing something right with their Mediterranean diet rich in olive oil. A burger might not exactly fit into those parameters, but I can use the salty, briny, and fresh elements that they love to make this burger Greek. Flavorful kalamata olives are blended into a spread for the bun, and this combo wouldn't be Greek without some salty feta cheese and ripe tomato. You might not be as familiar with tzatziki, but this tangy blend of thick yogurt, pungent garlic, and grated fresh cucumber is a staple in Greek cuisine and is used for practically everything, from a dip for wedges of pita bread and French fries to a topping for sandwiches.

**SERVES 4**

½ cup Greek yogurt
¼ cup grated cucumber
2 cloves garlic, finely chopped
Kosher salt and freshly ground
    black pepper
¾ cup pitted kalamata olives
2 teaspoons chopped fresh oregano leaves,
    plus more for garnish
2 tablespoons extra-virgin olive oil
1½ pounds ground chuck (80 percent lean)
    or ground turkey (90 percent lean)
1½ tablespoons canola oil
⅓ cup crumbled feta cheese, plus sliced
    feta cheese, for garnish (optional)
4 hamburger buns, split; toasted
    (see page 15), if desired
½ ripe beefsteak tomatoes, chopped

**1.** Whisk together the yogurt, cucumber, and garlic in a small bowl and season with salt and pepper. Refrigerate for at least 30 minutes or up to 8 hours before serving to allow the flavors to meld.

**2.** Combine the olives, oregano, and olive oil in a food processor and process until smooth. The olive paste can be made up to 1 day ahead, covered, and refrigerated. Bring to room temperature before using.

**3.** Divide the meat into 4 equal portions (about 6 ounces each). Form each portion loosely into a ¾-inch-thick burger and make a deep depression in the center with your thumb. Season both sides of each burger with salt and pepper.

**4.** Cook the burgers, using the canola oil (see page 16) and topping each one with crumbled feta cheese and a basting cover during the last minute of cooking (see page 21).

**5.** Place the burgers on the bun bottoms, and spoon some of the yogurt sauce and olive paste over the burgers. Top with chopped tomato, sliced feta, if desired, and oregano. Cover with the bun tops, and serve immediately.

# LOUISIANA BURGER

Louisiana, and in particular the city of New Orleans, is known for its amazing food. One technique that the local chefs there have mastered is blackening, a method by which a piece of chicken, fish, or steak is coated in a peppery crust and quickly cooked over very high heat to—well—blacken the exterior. The Louisiana burger applies this method to a burger. (If you don't want to take it all the way to black, you can do something called "bronzing," which follows the same principle as blackening but does so to a lesser degree of darkness.) Blackening is best done in a cast-iron pan. I based the condiment for this burger on the classic New Orleans rémoulade sauce; it incorporates so many of the things that I use on my burgers—such as mustard, hot sauce, mayonnaise, and pickles (sour cornichons, here)—into one delicious spread.

**SERVES 4**

## SPICY RÉMOULADE
½ cup mayonnaise
2 teaspoons Dijon mustard
2 teaspoons whole-grain mustard
½ teaspoon hot sauce
5 cornichons, diced
1 green onion, white and pale green
   parts, finely chopped
1 tablespoon finely chopped fresh
   flat-leaf parsley leaves
Kosher salt and freshly ground
   black pepper

## BURGERS
1 tablespoon sweet Spanish paprika
2 teaspoons freshly ground black pepper
2 teaspoons kosher salt
1 teaspoon dried thyme
½ teaspoon garlic powder
½ teaspoon onion powder
½ teaspoon cayenne pepper
1½ pounds ground chuck (80 percent lean)
   or ground turkey (90 percent lean)
1½ tablespoons canola oil
1 red onion, cut into ¼-inch-thick slices
4 hamburger buns, split; toasted
   (see page 15), if desired

**1.** To make the rémoulade, whisk together the mayonnaise, Dijon and whole-grain mustards, hot sauce, cornichons, green onion, and parsley in a small bowl and season with salt and pepper. Cover and refrigerate for at least 1 hour or up to 8 hours.

**2.** To make the spice rub for the burgers, stir together the paprika, black pepper, salt, thyme, garlic and onion powders, and cayenne in a small bowl.

**3.** Divide the meat into 4 equal portions (about 6 ounces each). Form each portion loosely into a ¾-inch-thick burger and make a deep depression in the center with your thumb. Season one side of each patty with the spice mixture, making sure to rub the spices into the meat.

**4.** Heat the oil in a sauté pan or griddle, preferably cast iron, over high heat until the oil begins to shimmer. Cook the burgers, spice side down, until they are slightly charred and the spices have formed a crust, about 1½ minutes (be careful not to burn the spices). Turn the burgers over, lower the heat to medium, and continue cooking until golden brown and slightly charred on the second side, about 4 minutes for medium rare or until cooked to the desired degree of doneness (see page 17 for approximate cooking times). Remove the burgers to a plate and tent loosely with aluminum foil.

**5.** Add the onion to the pan and cook over medium-high heat until slightly softened, about 2 minutes per side.

**6.** Put the burgers on the bun bottoms and top with the onion slices and some rémoulade sauce. Cover with the bun tops and serve immediately.

# MIAMI BURGER

A trip to Miami wouldn't be complete without stopping for an authentic Cuban sandwich, hot off the press and stuffed with roasted pork, smoked ham, garlicky mayonnaise, tangy mustard, dill pickles, and oozing Swiss cheese. It's almost enough to make you miss your flight home. Turning this Cuban specialty into an American one isn't hard to do: just replace the roasted pork with a good old hamburger. Pressing the assembled burger not only yields a crispy toasted bun, but also ensures that all of the elements meld into one cohesive, mouthwatering sandwich.
**SERVES 4**

  1 pound ground chuck (80 percent lean) or
      ground turkey (90 percent lean)
  Kosher salt and freshly ground black
      pepper
  1½ tablespoons canola oil
  ½ cup mayonnaise
  4 cloves roasted garlic (see page 78),
      mashed
  4 hamburger buns, split
  ¼ cup Dijon mustard
  8 thin slices Swiss cheese
  4 thin slices smoked ham
  2 dill pickles, sliced into ¼-inch-thick slices

**1.** Divide the meat into 4 equal portions (about 6 ounces each). Form each portion loosely into a ¾-inch-thick burger and make a deep depression in the center with your thumb. Season both sides of each burger with salt and pepper. Cook the burgers, using the oil (see page 16). Remove the burgers to a plate.

**2.** Combine the mayonnaise and roasted garlic in a small bowl and season with salt and pepper to taste. Spread both sides of each bun with the mayonnaise and the mustard. Place a slice of cheese on each bun bottom, place a burger on top, and then top the burger with a slice of ham, another slice of cheese, and some pickle slices. Cover with the bun tops.

**3.** Cook the burgers on a sandwich press or wrap the burgers in aluminum foil and cook in a hot skillet over high heat (put a heavy skillet on top of the burgers to press them), until golden brown and the cheese has melted, about 1½ minutes per side. Serve immediately.

# NAPA VALLEY BURGER

This burger could turn anyone into a West Coast convert with just one bite. Northern California's gorgeous Napa Valley is home to more than vineyards; it also produces some great local goat cheese and the Meyer lemon. Intriguingly sweet and far more mellow than the standard variety, Meyer lemons are a wonderful treat. Their season is short, however, and they can also be prohibitively expensive. But I still love that flavor and have found that I can replicate it with a mixture of fresh lemon and orange juices. The Meyer lemon–honey mustard is fresh and bright, not cloying. Its sweet note is a great counterpoint to the tangy goat cheese and crunchy, peppery watercress.

**SERVES 4**

### MEYER LEMON–HONEY MUSTARD

¼ cup Dijon mustard
1 heaping tablespoon clover honey
1½ teaspoons grated Meyer lemon zest,
　　or 1 teaspoon grated orange zest and
　　½ teaspoon grated lemon zest
1½ tablespoons Meyer lemon juice, or
　　1 tablespoon fresh orange juice and
　　1 teaspoon fresh lemon juice
Kosher salt and freshly ground
　　black pepper

### BURGERS

1½ pounds ground chuck (80 percent lean)
　　or ground turkey (90 percent lean)
Kosher salt and freshly ground
　　black pepper
1½ tablespoons canola oil

8 round slices fresh goat cheese,
　　each ½ inch thick
4 sesame seed hamburger buns, split;
　　toasted (see page 15), if desired
1 handful of watercress

**1.** To make the Meyer lemon–honey mustard, whisk together the mustard, honey, lemon zest, and lemon juice and season with salt and pepper. Cover and refrigerate for at least 30 minutes or up to 24 hours before serving to allow the flavors to meld.

**2.** Divide the meat into 4 equal portions (about 6 ounces each). Form each portion loosely into a ¾-inch-thick burger and make a deep depression in the center with your thumb. Season both sides of each burger with salt and pepper.

**3.** Cook the burgers, using the canola oil (see page 16) and topping each one with 2 slices of cheese and a basting cover during the last minute of cooking (see page 21).

**4.** Place the burgers on the bun bottoms, drizzle with some of the Meyer lemon–honey mustard, and top with watercress. Cover with the bun tops and serve immediately.

# NACHO BURGER

My love for the ingredients of the American Southwest is pretty well documented at this point, making this burger something of a signature. Cool and creamy avocados and spicy tomato-chipotle salsa make this burger a tribute to that region. Blue corn chips supply the crunch factor that lettuce would normally provide, but in a far tastier, more southwestern way. This couldn't be called "Nacho" without cheese; sliced Monterey Jack fills the bill perfectly.

**SERVES 4**

### TOMATO-CHIPOTLE SALSA
3 tablespoons red wine vinegar
1 tablespoon canola oil
2 teaspoons pureed canned chipotle chiles
   in adobo
3 plum tomatoes, seeded and finely diced
2 tablespoons finely diced red onion
2 tablespoons finely chopped fresh
   cilantro leaves
Kosher salt

### BURGERS
1½ pounds ground chuck (80 percent lean)
   or ground turkey (90 percent lean)
Kosher salt and freshly ground black
   pepper
1½ tablespoons canola oil
8 slices Monterey Jack cheese, each
   ¼ inch thick
4 hamburger buns, split; toasted
   (see page 15), if desired
Avocado Relish (page 34)

4 Pickled Jalapeños (page 115),
   thinly sliced
½ cup coarsely crumbled blue corn
   tortilla chips

**1.** To make the salsa, stir together the vinegar, oil, and chipotle puree in a medium bowl. Add the tomatoes, onion, and cilantro and mix to combine; season with salt. The salsa can be made 4 hours in advance, covered, and refrigerated. Bring to room temperature before using.

**2.** Divide the meat into 4 equal portions (about 6 ounces each). Form each portion loosely into a ¾-inch-thick burger and make a deep depression in the center with your thumb. Season both sides of each burger with salt and pepper.

**3.** Cook the burgers, using the canola oil (see page 16) and topping each one with 2 slices of cheese and a basting cover during the last minute of cooking (see page 21).

**4.** Place the burgers on the bun bottoms. Top each burger with some of the avocado relish, some tomato-chipotle salsa, and then pickled jalapeños and blue corn chips. Cover with the burger tops and serve immediately.

# OAXACAN BURGER

Oaxaca is a state in southern Mexico with a diverse and celebrated regional cuisine. One of Oaxaca's best-known specialties is mole, a classic Mexican sauce that combines onions, tomatoes, chiles, fried corn tortillas, and often chocolate, which adds a rich, not sweet, deep note to the sauce. Traditionally, mole is time-consuming to make and involves many separate cooking techniques. This version is just as tasty as the original but is quick and easy to prepare. Tangy crumbled queso fresco, creamy slices of avocado, and pickled red onions provide the authentically Mexican finishing touches.

**SERVES 4**

## MOLE

¼ cup slivered almonds
2 tablespoons canola oil
1 small Spanish onion, coarsely chopped
2 cloves garlic, coarsely chopped
2 tablespoons ancho chile powder
1 tablespoon New Mexico chile powder
One 28-ounce can plum tomatoes and their juices, pureed
¼ cup crushed white or yellow corn tortilla chips
1 ounce semisweet or bittersweet chocolate, finely chopped
1 tablespoon honey
1 tablespoon pure maple syrup
Kosher salt and freshly ground black pepper

## BURGER

1½ pounds ground chuck (80 percent lean) or ground turkey (90 percent lean)
Kosher salt and freshly ground black pepper
1½ tablespoons canola oil
4 sesame seed hamburger buns, split; toasted (see page 15), if desired
2 ounces crumbled queso fresco (about ½ cup)
1 ripe Hass avocado, halved, pitted, peeled, and cut into 8 wedges
Pickled Red Onions (page 116; optional)

*(recipe continues)*

**1.** To make the mole, put the almonds in a medium saucepan over medium heat and toast, stirring occasionally, until lightly golden brown, about 5 minutes. Remove the almonds to a plate.

**2.** Increase the heat under the pan to high, add the oil, and heat until it begins to shimmer. Add the onion and cook until soft, about 4 minutes. Add the garlic and cook for 30 seconds. Stir in the ancho and New Mexico chile powders and cook for 1 minute. Add the tomato puree and almonds, bring to a boil, and cook, stirring occasionally, for 5 minutes. Add the tortilla chips and cook until the sauce is reduced by half, about 10 minutes.

**3.** Carefully transfer the mixture to a blender and blend until smooth. Return the mixture to the pan over high heat, add the chocolate, honey, and maple syrup, and cook until reduced to a sauce consistency, about 5 minutes. Season with salt and pepper and keep warm.

**4.** Divide the meat into 4 equal portions (about 6 ounces each). Form each portion loosely into a ¾-inch-thick burger and make a deep depression in the center with your thumb. Season both sides of each burger with salt and pepper. Cook the burgers, using the canola oil (see page 16).

**5.** Place the burgers on the bun bottoms and top each with some of the mole sauce, some queso fresco, 2 avocado wedges, and pickled onions, if using. Cover with the bun tops and serve immediately.

# PATTY MELT BURGER

The patty melt first appeared on the American diner scene in the 1940s and is still a favorite more than sixty years later. Take a good look at what it is—meat and cheese pressed between slices of buttered bread—and you might wonder: Was the patty melt America's first panini?

As a rule, my perfect burger consists of a thicker patty served on a soft roll, but everyone needs to break the rules, even their own, once in a while. This patty melt, with its sophisticated jam-like onion relish and buttery Gruyère cheese, makes breaking the rules extra delicious.

**SERVES 4**

### RED WINE ONION RELISH

2 tablespoons olive oil
2 medium red onions, halved and thinly sliced
Kosher salt and freshly ground black pepper
1 cup dry red wine
2 tablespoons red wine vinegar
2 tablespoons honey
2 teaspoons finely chopped fresh thyme leaves
2 tablespoons finely chopped fresh flat-leaf parsley leaves

### PATTY MELTS

1 pound ground chuck (80 percent lean) or ground turkey (90 percent lean)
Kosher salt and freshly ground black pepper
1 tablespoon canola oil
8 slices good-quality seeded rye bread, each ½ inch thick
8 tablespoons (1 stick) unsalted butter, softened
4 ounces Gruyère cheese, coarsely grated (about 1 cup)
4 Pickled Jalapeños (page 115), halved (optional)

*(recipe continues)*

**1.** To make the relish, heat the oil in a medium sauté pan over medium-low heat. Add the onions and season with salt and pepper. Cover the pan with a lid and cook the onions, stirring occasionally, until soft, about 10 minutes.

**2.** Increase the heat to medium-high and add the wine, vinegar, honey, and thyme and simmer, stirring occasionally, until the liquid evaporates and the mixture thickens to a jam-like consistency, 5 to 7 minutes. Transfer to a bowl, stir in the parsley, and let cool to room temperature. The relish can be made 2 days ahead and stored, covered, in the refrigerator. Bring to room temperature before using.

**3.** Divide the meat into 4 equal portions (about 4 ounces each). Form each portion loosely into a ½-inch-thick burger and make a deep depression in the center with your thumb. Season both sides of each burger with salt and pepper.

**4.** Heat the oil in a sauté pan or griddle, preferably cast iron, over high heat until the oil begins to shimmer. Cook the burgers until slightly charred and cooked to medium, about 3 minutes per side.

**5.** Butter 4 slices of the bread with 4 table-spoons of the butter. Turn the bread over (buttered side down) on a flat surface and divide half of the cheese over the top. Spoon half of the onion relish on top of the cheese, add the burgers, and then spoon on the remaining relish and cheese. Cover with the remaining 4 slices of bread and butter the tops with the remaining 4 tablespoons butter. Press down gently on the sandwiches.

**6.** Wipe out the pan with paper towels and heat it over medium heat. Cook the melts until the bread is golden brown and crispy and the cheese has melted, about 1½ minutes per side. Serve immediately, topped with pickled jalapeños, if desired.

# PHILADELPHIA BURGER

The first thing that I have to do on any visit to Philadelphia is get myself a cheesesteak. Whether it's from Tony Luke's, Gino's, or Pat's, I can't do anything until I've had one. I always order mine with Provolone cheese and lots of hot peppers, and you've got to do what the locals do and say "wit," as in with griddled sweet onions and bell peppers. All of those toppings do make for one great sandwich, but move them onto a burger . . . now that's what I'm talking about! And I don't even need to leave my home state to get my fix.

**SERVES 4**

3½ tablespoons canola oil
1 large Spanish onion, sliced into thin rings
1½ pounds ground chuck (80 percent lean) or ground turkey (90 percent lean)
Kosher salt and freshly ground black pepper
8 slices aged Provolone cheese, each ¼ inch thick
4 sesame seed hamburger buns, split; toasted (see page 15), if desired
2 jarred roasted red bell peppers, coarsely chopped
Pickled hot pepper rings
Fresh flat-leaf parsley leaves, for garnish (optional)

**1.** Heat 2 tablespoons of the canola oil in a sauté pan or griddle over medium-high heat until almost smoking. Add the onions and cook, stirring occasionally, until soft and lightly golden brown, about 20 minutes. Remove the onions to a plate.

**2.** Divide the meat into 4 equal portions (about 6 ounces each). Form each portion loosely into a ¾-inch-thick burger and make a deep depression in the center with your thumb. Season both sides of each burger with salt and pepper.

**3.** Cook the burgers, using the remaining 1½ tablespoons canola oil (see page 16) and topping each one with 2 slices of cheese and a basting cover during the last minute of cooking (see page 21).

**4.** Place the burgers on the bun bottoms and top with onions, roasted red peppers, hot peppers, and parsley, if using. Cover with the bun tops and serve immediately.

# SANTA FE BURGER

This is one seriously delicious cheeseburger inspired by the flavors of the Southwest, personal favorites of mine. A luscious, gooey queso sauce made with Monterey Jack cheese takes the place of sliced cheese and makes a secure bed for roasted and diced poblano chiles. Blue corn tortilla chips give the burger an unexpectedly perfect touch of salty crunch. The queso sauce would also be wonderful as a dip for chips or fries.

**SERVES 4**

### BURGERS
1 large poblano chile
2½ tablespoons canola oil
Kosher salt and freshly ground
    black pepper
1½ pounds ground chuck (80 percent lean)
    or ground turkey (90 percent lean)
4 hamburger buns, split; toasted
    (see page 15), if desired
12 blue or yellow corn tortilla chips

### QUESO SAUCE
1 tablespoon unsalted butter
1 tablespoon all-purpose flour
1½ cups whole milk
8 ounces Monterey Jack cheese, coarsely
    grated (about 2 cups)
Kosher salt and freshly ground
    black pepper

**1.** Preheat the oven to 375 degrees F.

**2.** Put the chile on a rimmed baking sheet, rub with 1 tablespoon of the oil, and season with salt and pepper. Roast in the oven until the skin of the chile is blackened, about 15 minutes. Remove the chile from the oven, place in a bowl, cover with plastic wrap, and let the chile steam for 15 minutes. Peel, stem, and seed the chile and then coarsely chop it.

**3.** To make the queso sauce, melt the butter in a small saucepan over medium heat. Whisk in the flour and cook for 1 minute. Add the milk, increase the heat to high, and cook, whisking constantly, until slightly thickened, about 5 minutes. Remove from the heat and whisk in the cheese until melted; season with salt and pepper. Keep warm.

**4.** Divide the meat into 4 equal portions (about 6 ounces each). Form each portion loosely into a ¾-inch-thick burger and make a deep depression in the center with your thumb. Season both sides of each burger with salt and pepper. Cook the burgers, using the remaining 1½ tablespoons oil (see page 16).

**5.** Place the burgers on the bun bottoms and top each with a few tablespoons of queso sauce, chips, and some of the poblano. Cover with the bun tops and serve immediately.

# TRATTORIA BURGER

This burger gets its inspiration from Italy's *insalata caprese,* which is a simple yet totally delicious layering of fresh mozzarella, ripe tomato slices, and basil leaves. Basically, I just transplant that salad onto a burger. Because it is so simple, it is of the utmost importance that each ingredient be in its prime. That means only the ripest, tastiest tomatoes, the freshest, creamiest mozzarella, and the brightest green basil will do. (If you can find it, make this burger with milky buffalo mozzarella for a delicious and authentically Italian treat.) All it takes to dress this Italian trifecta is a splash of balsamic vinegar, olive oil, salt, and lots of freshly ground black pepper.

SERVES 4

  1½ pounds ground chuck (80 percent lean)
     or ground turkey (90 percent lean)
  Kosher salt and freshly ground
     black pepper
  1½ tablespoons canola oil
  8 ounces fresh whole-milk mozzarella,
     sliced into 8 slices
  4 hamburger buns, split; toasted
     (see page 15), if desired
  4 slices ripe beefsteak tomato
  8 fresh basil leaves
  8 teaspoons balsamic vinegar
  4 teaspoons extra-virgin olive oil

**1.** Divide the meat into 4 equal portions (about 6 ounces each). Form each portion loosely into a ¾-inch-thick burger and make a deep depression in the center with your thumb. Season both sides of each burger with salt and pepper.

**2.** Cook the burgers, using the canola oil (see page 16) and topping each one with 2 slices of cheese and a basting cover during the last minute of cooking (see page 21).

**3.** Place the burgers on the bun bottoms and top with sliced tomato and 2 basil leaves. Drizzle each burger with 2 teaspoons balsamic vinegar and 1 teaspoon olive oil, cover with the bun tops, and serve immediately.

# WILD MUSHROOM-CHEDDAR BURGER

During my travels for the old Food Network show *Food Nation,* I had the opportunity to go foraging for mushrooms with an expert while in Washington State. I can't think of mushrooms without remembering that trip. Now I do NOT recommend hunting for your own mushrooms—let's leave that to the experts—but I do recommend using a variety of what your supermarket has to offer. They may not be technically "wild," but a blend from your market will still be delicious and, more important, not deadly! I think that any cheddar would pair well with the mushrooms, but if you can find a sharp Tillamook cheddar from Oregon, it would be all the better.

**SERVES 4**

2 tablespoons olive oil
1 tablespoon unsalted butter
12 ounces assorted mushrooms (such as
    cremini, lobster, chanterelles, and
    stemmed shiitakes), chopped
1 small shallot, finely diced
Kosher salt and freshly ground
    black pepper
1 tablespoon chopped fresh thyme leaves
2 tablespoons chopped fresh flat-leaf
    parsley leaves
1½ pounds ground chuck (80 percent lean)
    or ground turkey (90 percent lean)
1½ tablespoons canola oil
4 slices sharp cheddar cheese
4 hamburger buns, split; toasted
    (see page 15), if desired
Chipotle Ketchup (page 112; optional)

**1.** Heat the olive oil and butter in a large sauté pan over high heat until almost smoking. Add the mushrooms and cook, stirring occasionally, until soft, about 5 minutes. Add the shallot, season with salt and pepper, and cook until the mushrooms are golden brown, about 5 minutes. Stir in the thyme and parsley and transfer to a bowl.

**2.** Divide the meat into 4 equal portions (about 6 ounces each). Form each portion loosely into a ¾-inch-thick burger and make a deep depression in the center with your thumb. Season both sides of each burger with salt and pepper.

**3.** Cook the burgers, using the canola oil (see page 16) and topping each one with a slice of cheese and a basting cover during the last minute of cooking (see page 21).

**4.** Place the burgers on the bun bottoms and top each burger with chipotle ketchup, if using, and a large spoonful of the mushrooms. Cover with the bun tops and serve immediately.

# TURKEY COBB BURGER

Cobb salads occupy a delicious middle ground between the decadent (hello bacon and blue cheese!) and the virtuous (lean turkey, and it is a salad after all). Whichever side you land on, there is no denying how awesome the mixture of tangy blue cheese, salty bacon, creamy avocados, ripe tomatoes, and crisp romaine lettuce is. It's not hard to imagine how good those ingredients would taste not tossed with cubes of cold roasted turkey, but atop a hot and juicy turkey burger. It makes perfect sense to me!

**SERVES 4**

1 tablespoon red wine vinegar
1 tablespoon fresh lemon juice
1 teaspoon Dijon mustard
1 teaspoon Worcestershire sauce
1 clove garlic, finely chopped
Kosher salt and freshly ground
    black pepper
¼ cup extra-virgin olive oil
1½ pounds ground turkey (90 percent lean)
1½ tablespoons canola oil
2 ounces crumbled blue cheese
    (about ½ cup), plus more for garnish
    (optional)
4 hamburger buns, split; toasted
    (see page 15), if desired
1¼ cups finely shredded romaine lettuce
1 large ripe beefsteak tomato, cut into
    8 slices
1 ripe Hass avocado, halved, pitted, peeled,
    and sliced
8 slices crisp cooked bacon

**1.** To make the dressing, whisk together the vinegar, lemon juice, mustard, Worcestershire sauce, and garlic in a large bowl. Season with salt and pepper and then whisk in the olive oil.

**2.** Divide the meat into 4 equal portions (about 6 ounces each). Form each portion loosely into a ¾-inch-thick burger and make a deep depression in the center with your thumb. Season both sides of each burger with salt and pepper.

**3.** Cook the burgers, using the canola oil (see page 16) and topping each one with some of the cheese and a basting cover during the last minute of cooking (see page 21).

**4.** Place the burgers on the bun bottoms. Toss the romaine with the dressing and arrange over the burgers. Top each with 2 slices of bacon, 2 slices of tomato, sliced avocado, and additional blue cheese, if desired. Cover each burger with the bun tops and serve immediately.

# BLUE BURGER

I couldn't do this book without including a blue cheese and bacon burger; the combination of a juicy burger, crisp, smoky bacon, and sharp and tangy blue cheese is just too good. You can top this burger with crumbled blue cheese or you can do what I often do and spoon some hot Blue Cheese Sauce (page 110) over the finished burger. Serve it with warm Home-made Potato Chips (page 98) and extra sauce for dipping; it's insanely delicious. (See photograph on page 2.)

**SERVES 4**

    8 slices double-smoked bacon, each
        ¼ inch thick
    1½ pounds ground chuck (80 percent lean)
        or ground turkey (90 percent lean)
    Kosher salt and freshly ground
        black pepper
    1½ tablespoons canola oil
    2 ounces blue cheese, crumbled
        (about ½ cup)
    Chopped fresh flat-leaf parsley leaves, for
        garnish (optional)
    4 hamburger buns, split; toasted
        (see page 15), if desired

**1.** Cook the bacon in a large sauté pan over medium heat until golden brown and slightly crisp, 3 to 4 minutes per side. Remove the bacon to a plate lined with paper towels.

**2.** Divide the meat into 4 equal portions (about 6 ounces each). Form each portion loosely into a ¾-inch-thick burger and make a deep depression in the center with your thumb. Season both sides of each burger with salt and pepper.

**3.** Cook the burgers, using the oil (see page 16) and topping each one with some cheese and a basting cover during the last minute of cooking (see page 21).

**4.** Place the burgers on the bun bottoms and top each with 2 slices of bacon and chopped parsley, if using. Cover with the bun tops and serve immediately.

70

# SALMON BURGER WITH HOISIN BARBECUE SAUCE AND PICKLED GINGER AND NAPA SLAW

Hoisin is a sweet yet complex Chinese condiment that you can find in the Asian section of just about every supermarket these days. The hoisin-based barbecue sauce is especially delicious with rich salmon, but it would also be great on beef or turkey burgers. The pickled ginger and cabbage slaw, which contain quintessentially Asian ingredients such as garlic, rice wine vinegar, and toasted sesame oil, are an ideal way to add some fresh crunch to the burger.

**SERVES 4**

### HOISIN BARBECUE SAUCE

2 tablespoons canola oil
2 large shallots, coarsely chopped
2 cloves garlic, coarsely chopped
½ cup hoisin sauce
2 tablespoons ketchup
2 tablespoons honey
2 teaspoons soy sauce
2 teaspoons fish sauce
1 tablespoon rice wine vinegar

### SALMON BURGERS

1½ pounds fresh salmon
2 tablespoons canola oil
Kosher salt and freshly ground
  black pepper
4 hamburger buns, split; toasted
  (see page 15), if desired

### SLAW

2 tablespoons canola oil
¼ cup thinly sliced pickled ginger, plus
  more for garnish (optional)
2 cloves garlic, finely chopped
¼ small head of red cabbage,
  finely shredded
½ medium head of napa cabbage,
  finely shredded
Kosher salt and freshly ground
  black pepper
¼ cup rice wine vinegar
2 teaspoons toasted sesame oil
3 tablespoons finely chopped fresh
  cilantro leaves

*(recipe continues)*

**1.** To make the hoisin barbecue sauce, heat the oil in a medium saucepan over medium heat. Add the shallots and garlic and cook until soft, about 2 minutes. Add the hoisin, ketchup, honey, soy sauce, fish sauce, and vinegar and cook until heated through and slightly thickened, about 10 minutes. Set aside to cool. The sauce can be made 1 day in advance, covered, and refrigerated. Bring to room temperature before using.

**2.** To form the burgers, cut the salmon into large pieces and then coarsely chop in a food processor. Do not overprocess. (Alternatively you can chop it by hand with a sharp knife.) Divide the salmon into 4 equal portions (about 6 ounces each). Form each portion loosely into a ¾-inch-thick burger and make a deep depression in the center with your thumb. Place on a plate, cover with plastic wrap, and let chill in the refrigerator for at least 30 minutes before cooking.

**3.** Meanwhile, make the slaw. Heat the oil in a large sauté pan over high heat. Add the ginger and garlic and cook, stirring once, until soft, about 1 minute. Stir in the cabbage, season with salt and pepper, and cook, stirring once, until slightly wilted, 3 to 4 minutes. Remove from the heat and stir in the vinegar, sesame oil, and cilantro. Let sit at room temperature.

**4.** To cook the burgers, heat the oil in a sauté pan or griddle (nonstick or cast iron) until it begins to shimmer. Season both sides of each burger with salt and pepper. Cook the burgers until golden brown on the bottom sides, about 3 minutes. Turn over, brush with some of the hoisin barbecue sauce, and continue cooking until medium-well, about 3 minutes longer.

**5.** Place the burgers on the bun bottoms, drizzle some hoisin barbecue sauce over them, and top with the slaw. Garnish with pickled ginger, if desired. Cover with the burger tops and serve immediately.

# SALMON BURGER WITH HONEY MUSTARD-DILL SAUCE

This luscious burger is really quite simple. Salmon and dill are a classic pairing, but if you aren't a fan of dill, try adding a few table-spoons of chopped fresh mint or tarragon in its place. Thin slices of red onion add a nice somewhat sharp note, and thickly sliced cucumber gives the burger a refreshing crunch. Should you feel like experimenting with a different type of bun, pumpernickel rolls or bread would be a great choice.

**SERVES 4**

¼ cup Dijon mustard
1 tablespoon whole-grain mustard
3 tablespoons honey
3 tablespoons chopped fresh dill
Kosher salt and freshly ground black
    pepper
1½ pounds fresh salmon
2 tablespoons canola oil
4 hamburger buns, split; toasted
    (see page 15), if desired
12 slices English cucumber, each
    ¼ inch thick
½ small red onion, thinly sliced

**1.** Whisk together the Dijon and whole-grain mustards, honey, and dill in a small bowl and season with salt and pepper. Let the sauce sit for at least 30 minutes before serving. The sauce can be made 1 day in advance and stored, covered, in the refrigerator. Bring to room temperature before using.

**2.** Cut the salmon into large pieces and then coarsely chop in a food processor. Do not overprocess. (Alternatively you can chop it by hand with a sharp knife.) Divide the salmon into 4 equal portions (about 6 ounces each). Form each portion loosely into a ¾-inch-thick burger and make a deep depression in the center with your thumb. Place on a plate, cover with plastic wrap, and let chill in the refrigerator for at least 30 minutes before cooking.

**3.** Heat the oil in a sauté pan or griddle (nonstick or cast iron) until it begins to shim-mer. Season both sides of each burger with salt and pepper. Cook the burgers until golden brown on the bottom sides, about 3 minutes. Turn over and continue cooking until medium-well, about 3 minutes longer.

**4.** Place the burgers on the bun bottoms and top with slices of cucumber and onion. Drizzle the honey mustard–dill sauce over the top, cover with the burger tops, and serve immediately.

# TUNA BURGER WITH PINEAPPLE-MUSTARD GLAZE AND GREEN CHILE-PICKLE RELISH

This burger was a staple on Mesa Grill's lunchtime menu for years and it still makes a guest appearance from time to time. Tuna is a perfect choice for an alternative burger as its substantial meatiness really emulates that of beef. It also stands up to aggressive seasonings and is the perfect base for the slightly sweet, slightly tangy, slightly spicy pineapple-mustard glaze. The relish isn't like anything you'll get at a hot-dog stand; dill pickles, peppery poblano chiles, and tart lime juice make for a fresh, not sweet, crunchy relish.

**SERVES 4**

### PINEAPPLE-MUSTARD GLAZE
2 cups pineapple juice
¼ cup white wine vinegar
1 small shallot, coarsely chopped
2-inch piece of fresh ginger, peeled and finely chopped
3 tablespoons packed light brown sugar
2 tablespoons soy sauce
2 tablespoons Dijon mustard
3 tablespoons fresh lime juice
Kosher salt and freshly ground black pepper

### GREEN CHILE-PICKLE RELISH
2 poblano chiles
2 tablespoons canola oil
Kosher salt and freshly ground black pepper
3 medium dill pickles, finely diced
¼ cup finely chopped red onion
3 tablespoons fresh lime juice
1 tablespoon honey
3 tablespoons finely chopped fresh cilantro leaves
3 tablespoons extra-virgin olive oil

### TUNA BURGERS
1½ pounds fresh tuna
4 tablespoons canola oil
2 tablespoons Dijon mustard
1 tablespoon honey
2 teaspoons pureed canned chipotle chile in adobo
2 green onions (green and pale green parts), thinly sliced
Kosher salt and freshly ground black pepper
4 hamburger buns, split; toasted (see page 15), if desired
Pickled Red Onions (page 116), for garnish (optional)

*(recipe continues)*

**1.** To make the glaze, combine the pineapple juice, vinegar, shallot, and ginger in a small nonreactive saucepan and cook over medium heat until reduced by half, about 10 minutes. Transfer to a blender and blend until smooth.

**2.** Return the mixture to the saucepan, add the brown sugar, and cook over high heat, stirring occasionally, until slightly thickened, about 5 minutes. Remove from the heat and whisk in the soy sauce, mustard, and lime juice and season with salt and pepper. Transfer to a bowl and let cool to room temperature. The glaze can be made 1 day in advance and stored in a container with a tight-fitting lid in the refrigerator. Bring to room temperature before serving.

**3.** Meanwhile, to make the relish, preheat the oven to 375 degrees F.

**4.** Put the chiles on a rimmed baking sheet, rub them with the oil, and season with salt and pepper. Roast in the oven until the skins of the chiles are blackened, about 15 minutes. Remove the chiles from the oven, place in a bowl, cover with plastic wrap, and let the chiles steam for 15 minutes. Peel, stem, and seed the chiles and then finely dice them.

**5.** Combine the chiles, pickles, onion, lime juice, honey, cilantro, and oil in a medium bowl and season with salt and pepper. Let sit at room temperature for 30 minutes before serving so that the flavors meld. The relish can be made 8 hours in advance and stored in a container with a tight-fitting lid in the refrigerator. Let come to room temperature before serving.

**6.** Cut the tuna into large pieces and then coarsely chop in a food processor. Do not overprocess. (Alternatively you can chop it by hand with a sharp knife.)

**7.** Whisk together 2 tablespoons of the oil, the mustard, honey, and chipotle in a large bowl. Add the tuna and green onions and gently fold to combine. Divide the tuna mixture into 4 equal portions (about 6 ounces each). Form each portion loosely into a ¾-inch-thick burger and make a deep depression in the center with your thumb. Place on a plate, cover with plastic wrap, and let chill in the refrigerator for at least 30 minutes before cooking.

**8.** To cook the burgers, heat the remaining 2 tablespoons oil in a sauté pan or griddle (nonstick or cast iron) until it begins to shimmer. Season both sides of each burger with salt and pepper. Cook the burgers until golden brown on the bottom sides, about 3 minutes. Turn over, brush with some of the glaze, and continue cooking until medium, about 3 minutes longer.

**9.** Place the burgers on the bun bottoms, drizzle with more of the glaze, and top with the relish and pickled red onions, if using. Cover with the burger tops and serve immediately.

# PROVENÇAL TUNA BURGER WITH ROASTED GARLIC-TOMATO AIOLI

This flavorful tuna burger is fully inspired by the niçoise salad from the Provence region of France. I do make an exception to my "no-add-ins" rule when forming the patties for fish burgers because the fish is generally so lean that it benefits from some additional moisture. Many of the salad's key components, such as briny and salty capers, niçoise olives, and anchovies (here in paste form), are mixed into the tuna burger itself along with sharp Dijon mustard, sweet shallots, and fresh basil. These ingredients also act as a binder, holding the burger together as it cooks. Roasting the garlic and tomato gives a deep yet mellow sweetness, while fresh lemon juice and zest supply a bright note to the full-flavored aioli. It's an elegant take on a burger.

SERVES 4

### ROASTED GARLIC-TOMATO AIOLI

4 cloves garlic, peeled
1 ripe plum tomato
2 tablespoons olive oil
Kosher salt and freshly ground
    black pepper
1 teaspoon grated lemon zest
1 tablespoon fresh lemon juice
1 teaspoon fresh thyme leaves
¾ cup mayonnaise

### TUNA BURGERS

1½ pounds fresh tuna
4 tablespoons olive oil
1 tablespoon mayonnaise
1 tablespoon Dijon mustard
1 tablespoon anchovy paste
1 teaspoon white wine vinegar
¼ cup chopped pitted niçoise olives
1 large shallot, finely chopped
1 tablespoon drained capers
¼ cup finely chopped fresh basil leaves
Kosher salt and freshly ground
    black pepper
4 French baguette rolls or hamburger rolls,
    split; toasted (see page 15), if desired
1 handful of mesclun greens

**1.** To make the aioli, preheat the oven to 375 degrees F.

**2.** Place the garlic and tomato on a rimmed baking sheet, toss with the oil, and season with salt and pepper. Roast in the oven until the tomato is soft and the garlic is light golden brown, about 15 minutes. Slice the tomato in half crosswise and remove the seeds. Set aside to cool.

**3.** Combine the garlic, tomato, lemon zest, lemon juice, thyme, and mayonnaise in a food processor and process until smooth; season with salt and pepper. Cover and refrigerate for at least 30 minutes to allow the flavors to meld. The aioli can be made up to 8 hours in advance and stored in an airtight container in the refrigerator.

**4.** Cut the tuna into large pieces and then coarsely chop in a food processor. Do not overprocess. (Alternatively you can chop it by hand with a sharp knife.)

**5.** Whisk together 2 tablespoons of the oil, the mayonnaise, mustard, anchovy paste, vinegar, olives, shallot, and capers in a large bowl. Add the tuna and basil and gently fold to combine. Divide the tuna mixture into 4 equal portions (about 6 ounces each). Form each portion loosely into a ¾-inch-thick burger and make a deep depression in the center with your thumb. Place on a plate, cover with plastic wrap, and let chill in the refrigerator for at least 30 minutes before cooking.

**6.** To cook the burgers, heat the remaining 2 tablespoons oil in a sauté pan or griddle (nonstick or cast iron) until it begins to shimmer. Season both sides of each burger with salt and pepper. Cook the burgers until golden brown on the bottom sides, about 3 minutes. Turn over and continue cooking until medium, about 3 minutes longer.

**7.** Spread the aioli on both sides of the rolls and place the burgers and mesclun greens on the bottom halves. Cover with the roll tops and serve immediately.

# B

# FRENCH FRIES, POTATO CHIPS, AND ONION RINGS

PERFECT FRENCH FRIES 86 BISTRO FRENCH FRIES 88
GRILLED STEAK FRIES 91 OVEN-ROASTED FRIES 92
SWEET POTATO FRIES 95 PLANTAIN SHOESTRING FRIES 96
SHOESTRING FRIES 98 HOMEMADE POTATO CHIPS 98
BEER-BATTERED ONION RINGS 99 BUTTERMILK ONION RINGS 101

# FRENCH-FRY ESSENTIALS

**IT IS QUITE POSSIBLE THAT FRENCH FRIES MIGHT BE MORE POPULAR THAN BURGERS. CAN YOU THINK OF ANYONE WHO DOESN'T LIKE A GOOD BATCH OF FRIES? WHAT EXACTLY MAKES A FRENCH FRY GOOD IS MORE OPEN TO DEBATE.**

Some prefer their fries pale yellow and crispy, some golden brown and soft, some dark brown and crispy. Some like them thin, some fat, skin on, skin off, fried in vegetable oil, fried in peanut oil. Seasoned with just salt, seasoned with a variety of spices. Eaten plain or dipped in ketchup or mustard or mayonnaise or a combination of all three . . . the humble French fry has some opinionated fans! I offer up a few varieties in this book, but my perfect French fry is not too thick, not too thin, not too crispy, not too soft, not too pale, not too dark—I guess you could say it is *just right!*

I do have some definite tips to share for making fries that are just right. I am constantly asked the secret to making restaurant-style French fries at home by people who are frustrated by their own failed attempts. They complain of pale and oily fries or, on the complete other end of the spectrum, fries that

inevitably turn out overly dark and beyond crispy. There are a few rules to follow on your road to the perfect French fry, and I guarantee that if you do follow them, you will be turning out French fries that could compete with those of any restaurant out there.

I learned how to make fries while a student at the French Culinary Institute in New York City, but I perfected the technique while working at Jonathan Waxman's American bistro Jams, which he owned in the 1980s. He was a mentor to me in many ways, and among his many talents was his skill at turning out delicious and addictive French fries. Between his tutelage, my courses at FCI, and, perhaps most important, my own years of trial and error in the kitchen, I have come to the following conclusions as to what it takes to make a great French fry.

## POTATOES

French fries need to be made with a high-starch potato, not a waxy potato. To create the light, airy interior texture that provides such a wonderful contrast to the fry's crispy exterior, smart cooks use what food scientists call, for lack of a more appealing term, "mealy potatoes." Russets, the typical American baking potato, are an example of this variety. When cooked, the cells of mealy potatoes remain separate and distinct, while the cells of the equally unappealingly named "waxy potatoes" become clumped together. Because of this difference, fries made from mealy potatoes have a delicate, fluffy texture while fries made from the waxy variety are mushy and dense. In my opinion, there is only one potato that yields superior results every time: the Russet (also known as Idaho) potato. This brown-skinned, white-fleshed tuber contains less water than other potato varieties. This is what allows them to stay light and fluffy in the center with a crispy exterior, while absorbing very little oil.

## PEELED OR NOT PEELED

I generally prefer my fries without the skin and therefore peel my potatoes before cutting them. However, if you prefer yours with the skin left on, then by all means keep it on.

## FRY SIZE

As I mentioned above, there are many opinions on the size of the perfect fry. My personal preference is to cut each potato lengthwise into ¼-inch-thick slices and then slice again lengthwise into ¼-inch-square fries that are 3½ to 4 inches long.

## SOAKING

Soaking the cut potatoes in cold water for several hours before frying is probably the most important step. It removes a lot of the starch, which if left in the potatoes may cause them to stick together. Starch contains a lot of sugar and that sugar will also prevent the fries from getting crispy and cause them to brown too quickly on the outside. In my restaurants, we soak the sliced potatoes in the refrigerator for 8 hours or longer to remove as much starch as possible. If you don't have the time to soak for that long and need your French-fry fix immediately, you can cut the time down, but not to less than an hour. It is extremely important that the potatoes be drained well and patted dry with paper towels or kitchen towels before frying. Mixing water and hot oil is extremely dangerous; the water makes the oil bubble and splatter violently.

## EQUIPMENT

There is no need to buy a deep fryer to make homemade French fries. A tall heavy-bottomed stockpot works just fine. You will need a deep-fry thermometer, which can be found in any kitchen supply or home store and only costs a few bucks. You'll also want a spider, which is what chefs call a wire mesh strainer for removing the cooked fries from the oil. Crafted from durable steel with a nickel-plate finish, the skimmer tolerates high temperatures while the long handle ensures that hands are a safe distance away from the hot oil used for frying. The mesh head enables the excess oil to drain away so the food is not overly greasy.

While they are not necessary, tabletop deep fryers are notable for their safety. The simple fact that the hot oil is self-contained reduces many of the safety concerns that arise when frying on a stovetop, such as splattering. The tabletop fryers that I used in testing the recipes for this chapter made a convert out me; before this point I didn't see much of a middle ground between the commercial deep fryers that we use in the restaurants and, well, everything else, and I did all of my at-home frying on my stovetop. But I had tremendous success with both the Waring Pro Professional deep fryer and the Oster Cool Zone deep fryer and have reconsidered my frying ways. Beyond the safety issue, deep fryers are simple to use and produce a consistently good result. The models I liked heated the oil incredibly quickly to the temperature set on the self-controlled thermometer—another huge bonus. The oil also retained its heat well and, if needed, adjustments to the oil's temperature were easy to make and quick to take place. You can find the Waring Pro Professional and the Oster Cool Zone in many home stores and online, and both can be purchased for less than $150. If you love fried food (and, really, who doesn't!), they make a good investment.

## OIL

My preference is peanut oil, which has a high smoking point and yields a really crisp fry, but vegetable oil or canola oil will work just as well. Olive oil is not suitable for frying because of both its overly assertive taste and its relatively low smoking point; it will begin to burn before it gets hot enough to produce a crispy fry. The oil should be 3 inches deep in the pot. It can be reused two times for fries and once for onion rings. Let it cool completely, strain it well, and store it in the refrigerator. I wouldn't keep it for more than 1 week—and I don't recommend frying potato chips or fries in oil that you used to fry onions or your fries will taste like, well, onions.

## FRYING

Two stages of frying are required to yield a perfect result. Both stages should be done in batches. Adding too many fries at one time will cause the potatoes to stick together and to cook unevenly. The first stage is called blanching. Blanching means to cook quickly and this process does a few different things: it removes even more of the starch (which will make a crisper fry) and allows the inside of the potato to begin cooking. I prefer a temperature of 325 degrees F with a cooking time of 3 to 4 minutes, or until the potatoes are limp and a pale blond color. The potatoes should be drained well and transferred to paper towels or brown paper bags to drain and cool.

After all of your fries have been blanched, which can happen up to 8 hours in advance of serving (keep them at room temperature), heat the oil to 375 degrees F for the second step of frying. Finish the fries by frying in the hot oil until golden brown and crispy, 3 to 4 minutes. Drain again on clean paper towels and season immediately with salt or any other seasoning of your choice. Needless to say, fries are best served hot.

## POTATO CHIPS

Unlike French fries, homemade potato chips only require one quick fry at 360 degrees F to achieve the perfect texture, and you can use just about any type of potato. The key to making really great potato chips is slicing the potatoes really thin, ideally $1/16$ inch. The thinner you can make them, the crispier they will be.

## ONION RINGS

I prefer my onion rings sliced on the thicker side, about ¾ inch. Buy the biggest onions you can find and cut them into very thick rings. The bigger the onion and the thicker the ring, the fewer you have to prep. Remove the papery thin membrane covering the inside of each ring; this is very important. If you don't, the coating will adhere to the membrane rather than the ring and may fall off during frying. I like the contrast of a sweet onion against a crisp and salty coating, and I use the sweetest onions I can get my hands on for my rings. Vidalia onions are my top choice, but Walla Walla, Oso Sweet, and Maui onions are also all very sweet and very good, as are those labeled Bermuda onions. That being said, you can't go wrong with an onion ring made from a Spanish yellow onion, either. Basically, you just want it to be large, mild, and on the sweet side.

# PERFECT FRENCH FRIES

The name pretty much says it all: these are everything you could want from a French fry. They are great as is, but if you are looking for a change of pace, try tossing the fries with any of the seasoning mixtures on pages 117 to 119 or serving them with any of the condiments on pages 107 to 112.

**SERVES 4**

5 large Russet potatoes, peeled or well
    scrubbed, if leaving the skin on
1 quart peanut oil
Kosher salt

**1.** Cut the potatoes lengthwise into ¼-inch-thick slices, then cut each slice lengthwise into ¼-inch-thick fries. Put the fries in a large bowl of cold water and refrigerate for at least 1 hour and up to 8 hours.

**2.** Heat the oil in a heavy-bottomed medium stockpot over medium heat, or in a tabletop deep fryer, to 325 degrees F. Line a baking sheet with paper towels and set aside.

**3.** Drain the fries well and pat dry in batches with paper towels. Fry each batch, turning frequently, for 3 to 4 minutes or until the fries are a pale blond color and limp. Remove with a mesh skimmer to the baking sheet lined with paper towels.

**4.** Increase the heat of the oil to 375 degrees F.

**5.** Fry the potatoes again, in batches, turning frequently, until golden brown, 3 to 4 minutes. Remove with the skimmer and drain on clean paper towels. Season immediately with salt and serve hot.

# BISTRO FRENCH FRIES

These aromatic fries are often seen in bistros, where they accompany anything from steak to mussels to . . . that's right, a burger. These are garlicky to be sure, but not overwhelmingly so because the heat of the hot fries gently cooks the chopped garlic when the two are tossed together. Flecks of parsley bring a touch of bright color and flavor to the finished dish.

**SERVES 4 TO 6**

4 cloves garlic, finely chopped
¼ cup fresh flat-leaf parsley leaves,
    finely chopped
5 large Russet potatoes, peeled or well
    scrubbed, if leaving the skin on
1 quart peanut oil
Kosher salt

**1.** Combine the garlic and parsley in a small bowl.

**2.** Cut the potatoes lengthwise into ¼-inch-thick slices, then cut each slice lengthwise into ¼-inch-thick fries. Put the fries in a large bowl of cold water and refrigerate for at least 1 hour and up to 8 hours.

**3.** Heat the oil in a heavy-bottomed medium stockpot over medium heat, or in a tabletop deep fryer, to 325 degrees F. Line a baking sheet with paper towels and set aside.

**4.** Drain the fries well and pat dry in batches with paper towels. Fry each batch, turning frequently, for 3 to 4 minutes or until the fries are a pale blond color and limp. Remove with a mesh skimmer to the baking sheet lined with paper towels.

**5.** Increase the heat of the oil to 375 degrees F.

**6.** Fry the potatoes again, in batches, turning frequently, until golden brown, 3 to 4 minutes. Remove with the skimmer and drain on clean paper towels. Season immediately with salt, toss with the garlic-parsley mixture, and serve hot.

# GRILLED STEAK FRIES

It's nice to have the option to deliver a full meal straight off of the grill, fries and all. Though not as crispy as the deep-fried variety, these hearty grilled steak fries are every bit as satisfying. It's vital to grill the potato slices with the skin on; the skin not only provides an extra textural dimension, but also keeps the potatoes from falling apart on the grill. You can simply season these with salt and pepper or use any of the seasoning mixtures for fries (pages 117 to 119), if you so desire.
SERVES 4

    6 large Russet potatoes, scrubbed
    Kosher salt
    ¼ cup canola oil
    Freshly ground black pepper

**1.** Put the potatoes in a pot of cold water, add 2 tablespoons salt, and bring to a boil over medium-high heat. Cook the potatoes until they are tender when pierced with a knife but still firm, about 25 minutes. Drain, let cool, and then cut each potato lengthwise into 8 slices. This can be done in advance; the potatoes can be kept at room temperature for up to 4 hours or refrigerated for up to 8 hours.

**2.** Heat your grill to high.

**3.** Brush the potatoes with the oil and season with salt and pepper. Grill until golden brown and cooked through, 2 to 3 minutes per side. Serve hot.

# OVEN-ROASTED FRIES

Rich and buttery Yukon Golds are my potato of choice when making these substantial fries, but you can definitely use Russets if you'd rather. Should you decide to season the oven fries with one of the seasoning mixes, do so *before* roasting. The flavor of the spices will deepen with baking and give the fries a really great texture.

**SERVES 4**

5 large Yukon Gold potatoes, well scrubbed
¼ cup canola oil
1 tablespoon kosher salt
3 tablespoons seasoning mix (pages 117 to 119; optional)

**1.** Preheat the oven to 400 degrees F. Place a large rimmed baking sheet in the oven to heat for 10 minutes.

**2.** Meanwhile, slice each potato lengthwise into 8 slices. Put the potato slices in a large bowl, add the oil, salt, and seasoning mix, if using, and toss to coat the potatoes evenly.

**3.** Remove the baking sheet from the oven and add the potatoes in an even layer. Bake the potatoes, turning occasionally, until golden brown and cooked through, about 35 minutes. Serve hot.

# SWEET POTATO FRIES

I happen to love sweet potatoes and think they are great fried. One thing that you have to keep in mind when making this recipe is that sweet potato fries will never, ever be as crispy as fries made with regular potatoes; blanching them in oil or extending the soaking time won't change that. Sweet potatoes are very high in sugar and this keeps them from getting crisp. Their sugar content also makes them darken faster than standard potatoes, so don't walk away from the pot when making them! I prefer my sweet potato fries with the skin on, but if that's not to your liking feel free to peel them. For an extra hit of flavor, try seasoning the hot fries with a few tablespoons of either the Barbecue Seasoning (page 117) or the Mediterranean Seasoning (page 118).

**SERVES 4**

5 large sweet potatoes
1 quart peanut oil
Kosher salt

**1.** Cut the potatoes lengthwise into ¼-inch-thick slices, then cut each slice lengthwise into ¼-inch-thick fries.

**2.** Heat the oil in a heavy-bottomed medium stockpot over medium heat, or in a tabletop deep fryer, to 365 degrees F. Line a baking sheet with paper towels and set aside.

**3.** Fry each batch until golden brown, 3 to 4 minutes. Remove to the baking sheet lined with paper towels and season immediately with salt. Serve hot.

# PLANTAIN SHOESTRING FRIES

Fried plantains are enjoyed throughout the Caribbean and Latin America. They are a savory—not sweet—treat and you will need to use the unripe green variety for these fries, both for their taste and for their firm texture. I season mine in a Cuban style with lime zest and cayenne to further emphasize their origin, or you can use the Cuban Seasoning on page 118. Needless to say, they are the perfect accompaniment to the Miami Burger (page 51)!

**SERVES 4 TO 6**

1 tablespoon kosher salt
2 teaspoons grated lime zest
¼ teaspoon cayenne pepper
5 cups peanut oil
4 green plantains

**1.** Stir together the salt, lime zest, and cayenne in a small bowl.

**2.** Heat the oil in a heavy-bottomed medium stockpot over medium heat, or in a tabletop deep fryer, to 375 degrees F. Line a baking sheet with paper towels and set aside.

**3.** While the oil is heating, peel the plantains. To peel plantains: use a sharp knife to cut off the top and bottom ends. With the tip of the knife, make one slit in the skin of the plantain from top to bottom. Run the plantain under cold water and use your thumb and fingers to work the peel away from the fruit, beginning at the slit. Cut ½ inch off the ends of each plantain, then slice the plantains lengthwise with a U-shaped peeler or a mandoline into very thin strips (about ⅛ inch thick). Cut each strip lengthwise into ⅛-inch-thick fries.

**4.** Fry in batches, turning frequently, until golden brown, about 45 seconds. Remove with a mesh skimmer to the baking sheet lined with paper towels and season immediately with the salt mixture. Serve hot.

# SHOESTRING FRIES

Thin and crispy, shoestring potatoes are like a cross between a French fry and a potato chip. Because the potato is sliced so thin, these cook in a matter of seconds and you won't need to soak them or cook them twice as you would regular French fries. Unless you have an incredibly sharp knife and your knife skills are borderline masterful, I suggest using a mandoline to cut the super-thin slices of potato. You can of course season these with any of the spice mixtures on pages 117 to 119, but if you really want to be decadent, try them with a drizzle of white truffle oil and some shaved Parmigiano-Reggiano—delicious!

**SERVES 4 TO 6**

1 quart peanut oil
4 large Russet potatoes, peeled
Kosher salt

**1.** Heat the oil in a heavy-bottomed medium stockpot over medium heat, or in a tabletop deep fryer, to 375 degrees F. Line a baking sheet with paper towels and set aside.

**2.** While the oil is heating, slice the potatoes lengthwise into ⅛-inch-thick slices. Then cut each slice into long ⅛-inch-thick strips.

**3.** Add the strips to the hot oil in batches, separating them with a mesh skimmer when they hit the oil. Fry, turning frequently, until golden brown, 60 to 90 seconds. Remove with the skimmer and drain on the baking sheet lined with paper towels. Season immediately with salt and serve hot.

# HOMEMADE POTATO CHIPS

I never turn my nose up at potato chips out of a bag—what's not to like? But there is something incredibly satisfying about making your own, and eating them when they are hot. Considering how easy homemade potato chips are to make, there's no reason to deny yourself this pleasure. Just make sure that the potatoes are uniformly cut into thin slices and that you salt them as soon as they come out of the fryer. Now I *like* these chips just plain out of the fryer, but I *love* them dipped into warm, tangy, gooey Blue Cheese Sauce (page 110).

**SERVES 4 TO 6**

1 quart peanut oil
4 large Russet potatoes
Kosher salt

**1.** Heat the oil in a heavy-bottomed medium stockpot over medium heat, or in a tabletop deep fryer, to 360 degrees F.

**2.** While the oil is heating, slice the potatoes lengthwise into ⅛-inch-thick slices. Place the potato slices on a baking sheet between layers of paper towels to make sure they are very dry before frying.

**3.** Fry the potatoes in small batches, turning once, until golden brown on both sides, about 90 seconds. Remove with a mesh skimmer and drain on clean paper towels. Season with salt immediately. Serve hot, preferably, or at room temperature.

# BEER-BATTERED ONION RINGS

Sometimes an onion ring is all about the sweet, tender onion, and sometimes the coating is given the chance to share the spotlight. Well, if you are looking for an onion ring that falls into the latter category, this is the one for you. Beer acts as a leavening agent, making for an extremely tender batter, and the deep malt flavor of dark beer makes this delicious to boot.

SERVES 4

2 large Vidalia or other sweet onions
1 quart peanut oil
1 12-ounce bottle dark beer
3 large eggs
1 cup plus 2 tablespoons all-purpose flour
Kosher salt and freshly ground
   black pepper

**1.** Peel the onions and slice them crosswise into 1-inch-thick slices. Separate each slice into individual rings and then remove the papery thin membrane covering the inside of each ring.

**2.** Heat the oil in a heavy-bottomed medium stockpot over medium heat, or in a tabletop deep fryer, to 375 degrees F. Line a baking sheet with paper towels and set aside.

**3.** While the oil is heating, whisk together the beer, eggs, and 2 tablespoons flour in a large bowl and season with salt and pepper. Put the remaining 1 cup flour in a shallow baking dish and season with salt and pepper.

**4.** Dredge the onion rings in the flour and tap off the excess. Working in batches, toss the onions in the beer batter and let the excess batter drip off. Fry the batch of rings, turning once or twice, until golden brown and tender, about 4 minutes. Remove with a mesh skimmer and drain on the baking sheet lined with paper towels. Season immediately with salt. Repeat until all of the onion rings have been cooked. Serve hot.

# BUTTERMILK ONION RINGS

Even people who think they don't like onions will fall for these onion rings, which are crispy on the outside and have a sweet, soft interior. Double dipping the onion rings helps to give them that extra-crunchy coating. I love the extra-sweet taste of Vidalia onions, but if you can't find them in your market, any other sweet variety or even good old yellow onions will work well, too.

**SERVES 4**

2 large Vidalia or other sweet onions
1 quart peanut oil
2 cups buttermilk
Kosher salt and freshly ground
    black pepper
4 cups all-purpose flour
½ teaspoon cayenne pepper

**1.** Peel the onions and slice them crosswise into 1-inch-thick slices. Separate each slice into individual rings and then remove the papery thin membrane covering the inside of each ring.

**2.** Heat the oil in a heavy-bottomed medium stockpot over medium heat, or in a tabletop deep fryer, to 375 degrees F. Line a baking sheet with paper towels and set aside.

**3.** While the oil is heating, put the buttermilk in a large baking dish and season liberally with salt and black pepper. Divide the flour between 2 large baking dishes and season each dish liberally with salt and pepper and ¼ teaspoon of the cayenne.

**4.** Working in batches, dredge some of the onion rings in one of the dishes of flour and tap off the excess. Dip the rings in the buttermilk, allow the excess to drain off, and then dredge the rings in the second dish of flour, making sure to coat the rings evenly. Tap off the excess and transfer the batch of coated rings to the hot oil. Fry the rings, turning once or twice, until golden brown and tender, about 4 minutes. Remove with a mesh skimmer and drain on the baking sheet lined with paper towels. Season immediately with salt. Repeat until all of the onion rings have been cooked. Serve hot.

## SHOESTRING ONION RINGS

If you're not into big onion rings, make crispy, crunchy, thin onion rings, which are great on their own or mounded on top of the Cheyenne Burger (page 39).

Peel 2 large Vidalia onions and cut crosswise into ¼-inch-thick slices. Separate each slice into individual rings and then remove as many of the papery thin membranes covering the inside of each ring as you can. Proceed as for Buttermilk Onion Rings, above.

# B

# CONDIMENTS AND SEASONINGS

BARBECUE SAUCE 107 RED CHILE MUSTARD 108
HONEY MUSTARD 109 HORSERADISH MUSTARD MAYONNAISE 109
BLUE CHEESE SAUCE 110 CHIPOTLE KETCHUP 112
MALT VINEGAR–TARRAGON AIOLI 112 HOMEMADE DILL PICKLES 113
PICKLED JALAPEÑOS 114 PICKLED RED ONIONS 116
ASIAN SEASONING 117 BARBECUE SEASONING 117
CUBAN SEASONING 118 SOUTHWESTERN SEASONING 118
MEDITERRANEAN SEASONING 118
THREE-PEPPERCORN SEASONING 119

# CONDIMENT AND SEASONING ESSENTIALS

**EVEN THE PERFECT BURGER AND THE PERFECT FRENCH FRY CAN BENEFIT FROM A LITTLE DRESSING UP NOW AND AGAIN, BUT IT HAS TO BE DONE WITH STYLE. THE ACTUAL BURGERS THAT I MAKE ARE VERY STRAIGHTFORWARD, CLEAN AND SIMPLE, AS ARE MY FRIES, ONION RINGS, AND CHIPS. TOPPINGS ALLOW ME TO GET CREATIVE, BUT I ALSO CRAM A LOT OF FLAVOR, COLOR, TEXTURE, AND EXCITEMENT INTO MY CONDIMENTS AND SEASONING BLENDS.**

Whatever you need to transform your burger from basic to spectacular, whether it be the tangy heat of pickled jalapeños or a slathering of horseradish mustard mayonnaise, you'll find the recipe in this chapter. Many of these recipes come together in minutes, but regardless of how long they take, the level of flavor that you'll find makes anything you could buy in the store seem downright weak by comparison.

Piping hot and simply salted French fries or onion rings may hit the spot, but sometimes I want to amp up their flavor with something that ties them to the inspiration of the burger they are accompanying; the seasoning blends here help me do just that. So Cheyenne Burger, meet your side of southwestern-seasoned fries. Or how about pairing the Miami Burger with golden fries flavored with a healthy dose of savory Cuban seasoning? It's a perfect match.

The seasoning blends here can be used to flavor far more than what comes out of your fryer; they can also be used as spice rubs for what might otherwise be mundane chicken breasts or fish steaks or fillets. (Of course, this *is* a burger book, so you might want to try them on your burgers, too!) I give a few suggestions as to alternative uses for the seasonings, but do with them what you will. I'm sure you'll find a way to put them to good use in your kitchen, be it for a meal of burgers and fries or not.

The same thing holds true for the spreads and sauces that comprise the condiment section of this chapter; the barbecue sauce may have been included with the Dallas Burger in mind, but that doesn't mean that it wouldn't be just as wonderful basted on grilled chicken or steak. These sauces are pretty multifaceted; what started out atop your burger might happily make its way into a dipping sauce for your fries or onion rings. There are no rules, no judgments—just let your taste buds take the reins.

# BARBECUE SAUCE

I created this barbecue sauce to top the Dallas and Cheyenne burgers (pages 37 and 39), but it's also an ideal dipping sauce for Perfect French Fries (page 86). After you've made this quick and easy sauce once, you'll want to slather it on grilled chicken, steak, pork chops . . . you might never go back to the bottled stuff.

**MAKES 1 CUP**

2 tablespoons canola oil
1 medium Spanish onion, coarsely chopped
3 cloves garlic, coarsely chopped
1 cup ketchup
1 heaping tablespoon Dijon mustard
1 tablespoon red wine vinegar
1 tablespoon Worcestershire sauce
1 canned chipotle chile in adobo, chopped
2 tablespoons ancho chile powder
1 tablespoon sweet Spanish paprika
2 tablespoons packed dark brown sugar
1 tablespoon honey
1 tablespoon molasses
Kosher salt and freshly ground
  black pepper

**1.** Heat the oil over medium-high heat in a heavy-bottomed medium nonreactive saucepan. Add the onion and cook until soft, 3 to 4 minutes. Add the garlic and cook for 1 minute. Add the ketchup and ⅓ cup water and bring to a boil. Lower the heat and simmer for 5 minutes.

**2.** Add the mustard, vinegar, Worcestershire, chipotle chile, ancho chile powder, paprika, brown sugar, honey, and molasses and bring to a simmer. Cook, stirring occasionally, for an additional 10 minutes, or until thickened.

**3.** Transfer the mixture to a food processor and puree until smooth. Season with salt and pepper to taste. Pour into a bowl and allow to cool at room temperature. The sauce will keep for 1 week in a tightly sealed container in the refrigerator. Bring to room temperature before using.

# RED CHILE MUSTARD

This mustard gets its heat and color from ancho chile powder. Ancho chiles are dried poblanos and they have a flavor that I describe as that of a spicy raisin. I do recommend that you look for this variety for its pure deep flavor and don't use a generic blend labeled "chile powder." Red chile mustard is great on any beef or turkey burger and also makes a tasty dipping sauce for fries and onion rings.

**MAKES APPROXIMATELY 1/3 CUP**

¼ cup Dijon mustard
1 heaping tablespoon whole-grain mustard
1 heaping tablespoon ancho chile powder

Whisk together the Dijon and whole-grain mustards, ancho powder, and 1 teaspoon water in a bowl until combined. Cover and refrigerate for at least 30 minutes before using. The sauce will keep for 1 week in a tightly sealed container in the refrigerator.

# HONEY MUSTARD

There are loads of prepared honey mustards on the market today; all you need to do is open the jar and spread some on your burger. Take a good look at the ingredient lists, however, and you will find that many of them contain more corn syrup than they do honey. To make sure I'm getting just what I want flavor-wise, I prefer to mix up my own using my favorite Dijon mustard and a good-quality mild honey.

**MAKES 1 CUP**

¾ cup Dijon mustard
¼ cup clover honey
Kosher salt and freshly ground
black pepper

Whisk together the mustard and honey in a small bowl and season with salt and pepper. Cover and refrigerate for at least 30 minutes to allow the flavors to meld. The sauce will keep for 1 week in a tightly sealed container in the refrigerator.

# HORSERADISH MUSTARD MAYONNAISE

You would typically find this sauce served alongside a thick cut of prime rib. The blend of mellow mayonnaise, pungent horseradish, and sharp Dijon mustard complements steak so well that it is no surprise that it does the same for a beef burger. A rich salmon burger would also take beautifully to the sauce. For a touch of extra flavor and color, try adding a few tablespoons of chopped fresh herbs such as chives, dill, or tarragon.

**MAKES 1/2 CUP**

¼ cup mayonnaise
2 tablespoons Dijon mustard
2 tablespoons drained prepared
horseradish
Kosher salt and freshly ground
black pepper

Whisk together the mayonnaise, mustard, and horseradish in a small bowl and season with salt and pepper. Cover and refrigerate for at least 30 minutes to allow the flavors to meld. The sauce can be prepared 1 day in advance and kept covered in the refrigerator.

# BLUE CHEESE SAUCE

Use this béchamel-based sauce as a dip for potato chips and French fries or as a topping for burgers, such as the Buffalo Burger (page 27) or the Blue Burger (page 70).
**MAKES ABOUT 2 CUPS**

2 cups whole milk, or more, if needed
2 tablespoons unsalted butter
1 small Spanish onion, finely chopped
2 tablespoons all-purpose flour
¼ teaspoon kosher salt
Pinch of cayenne pepper
4 ounces crumbled blue cheese
    (about 1 cup), plus extra for garnish
2 tablespoons finely chopped fresh chives

**1.** Pour the milk into a small saucepan and bring to a simmer over low heat.

**2.** Heat the butter in a medium saucepan over medium heat. Add the onion and cook until soft, about 5 minutes. Stir in the flour and cook for 1 minute. Slowly whisk in the warm milk and continue whisking until the mixture thickens, about 2 minutes. Season with the salt and cayenne pepper and continue cooking, whisking occasionally, for 5 minutes.

**3.** Remove from the heat and stir in the cheese. If the sauce is too thick, thin with a little extra milk. The sauce can be prepared 1 day in advance, covered, and refrigerated. Reheat gently in a double boiler. Sprinkle with the chives.

# CHIPOTLE KETCHUP

I love ketchup as much as the next American does, but when I was designing the menu for Bobby's Burger Palace, I knew that I wanted to have a little something extra to offer in the squeeze bottles. The simple addition of pureed chipotle in adobo gives prepared ketchup an exciting smoky edge, while still keeping its sweet yet tangy identity intact.

**MAKES 1 CUP**

1 cup ketchup
2 to 3 tablespoons pureed canned chipotle in adobo (depending on how spicy you prefer it)
¼ teaspoon kosher salt
¼ teaspoon freshly ground black pepper

Whisk together the ketchup, chipotle, salt, and pepper in a small bowl. Cover and refrigerate for at least 30 minutes to allow the flavors to meld. The sauce will keep for 1 week in a tightly sealed container in the refrigerator.

# MALT VINEGAR– TARRAGON AIOLI

This aioli is a riff on a tartar sauce that I made for the fish and chips episode of my show *Throwdown*. I may not have won that particular battle, but I did come out of it with some good ideas. Fries taste delicious doused with malt vinegar, no question, but they can quickly become soggy. This aioli, fragrant with anise-flavored tarragon, blends the great taste of malt vinegar into a creamy dip for fries with even more flavor than the original combo, and none of the sogginess.

**MAKES ABOUT ⅔ CUP**

½ cup mayonnaise
1½ tablespoons malt vinegar
2 tablespoons finely chopped fresh tarragon leaves
Kosher salt and freshly ground black pepper

Whisk together the mayonnaise, vinegar, and tarragon in a bowl. Season with salt and pepper to taste. Cover and refrigerate for at least 30 minutes and up to 8 hours before serving.

# HOMEMADE DILL PICKLES

As a New Yorker, I have ready access to some of the best dill pickles out there. Even so, I still like to whip up a batch of my own every now and then. It is really very easy to do, and you have total control over the flavor and seasonings. If you really like garlic, toss in a few more cloves; if you prefer your pickles on the spicy side, add a couple of pinches of red pepper flakes. This is a basic recipe and you should feel free to experiment with other spices, too, such as cumin or fennel seeds. One note: though light on labor, this is not a last-minute recipe. The cucumbers need to "pickle" for at least 24 hours to get the best flavor.

**MAKES ABOUT 1 QUART**

4 Kirby cucumbers
¾ cup plus 2 tablespoons distilled
   white vinegar
¼ cup packed coarsely chopped fresh dill
2 tablespoons sugar
3 cloves garlic, coarsely chopped
1 tablespoon kosher salt
¾ teaspoon dill seeds
1 teaspoon whole mustard seeds
1 teaspoon coriander seeds

**1.** Slice the cucumbers into ¼-inch-thick slices. Put the cucumber slices in a medium bowl that has a fitted lid or in another lidded container that is large enough to hold them.

**2.** Combine 1 cup water, the vinegar, chopped dill, sugar, garlic, salt, dill seeds, mustard seeds, and coriander seeds in a small non-reactive saucepan and bring to a boil over high heat. Cook until the sugar and salt dissolve, about 2 minutes. Remove from the heat and let cool to room temperature.

**3.** Pour the mixture over the cucumbers, cover, and refrigerate for at least 24 hours or up to 1 week, stirring the mixture at least once during this time. Drain before serving, discarding the liquid and aromatics.

# PICKLED JALAPEÑOS

I love the spicy, vinegary punch of pickled jalapeño chiles. There's no need to reserve these for nachos only; this pickle goes well with any Mexican- or Southwestern-inspired dish—and that includes burgers—that could use an acidic touch of heat. It's simple to make your own, and I think you'll find that the freshness of home-pickled jalapeños beats any jarred or canned supermarket version, hands down.

**MAKES 15 PICKLED JALAPEÑOS**

15 jalapeño chiles
2 cups red wine vinegar
2 cups white wine vinegar
2 tablespoons kosher salt
2 tablespoons sugar
½ teaspoon coriander seeds
½ teaspoon black peppercorns
½ teaspoon fennel seeds
½ teaspoon mustard seeds
½ teaspoon cumin seeds

**1.** Bring a medium pan of salted water to a boil. Add the jalapeños to the water and blanch for 2 minutes. Drain well, pat dry with paper towels, and let cool slightly. Using a small paring knife, make a small slit in the center of each jalapeño and place in a small nonreactive bowl that has a tight-fitting lid.

**2.** Combine the red and white wine vinegars, the salt, sugar, coriander seeds, peppercorns, fennel seeds, mustard seeds, and cumin seeds in a medium nonreactive saucepan and bring to a boil over high heat. Cook until the sugar and salt dissolve, about 2 minutes. Remove from the heat and let cool to room temperature.

**3.** Pour the mixture over the jalapeños, cover, and refrigerate for at least 24 hours and up to 1 week, stirring the mixture at least once during this time. Drain before serving, discarding the liquid and aromatics.

# PICKLED RED ONIONS

Pickled onions such as these are most often used as a garnish for tacos, burritos, and guacamole in Mexican cuisine. I think they are just as delicious on most of the burgers in this book, and they add a level of intrigue that raw onion slices could never do. The fresh lime juice is essential for its fresh, clean flavor as well as its acidity. If you want to pump up the volume on flavor and add a bit of heat, try adding a few whole jalapeño or serrano chiles to the mix.

**MAKES ABOUT 2 CUPS**

1 cup fresh lime juice
½ cup distilled white vinegar
1 tablespoon sugar
2 teaspoons kosher salt
2 large red onions
2 teaspoons finely chopped fresh
    oregano leaves
2 whole serrano chiles or jalapeño chiles,
    slit down the center (optional)

**1.** Whisk together the lime juice, vinegar, sugar, and salt in a medium nonreactive bowl and let sit until the salt and sugar dissolve, about 5 minutes.

**2.** Meanwhile, peel and halve the onions, and then cut into ⅛-inch-thick slices. Add the onions, oregano, and chiles, if using, to the lime juice mixture and stir well to combine. Cover and refrigerate for at least 24 hours and up to 2 days, stirring the mixture at least once during this time. Drain before serving.

# ASIAN SEASONING

If you're looking for something to accompany an Asian-inspired burger, look no further. Whether used on French fries, potato chips, or onion rings, this seasoning blend infuses your dish with an Asian flair. Ultimately savory, it achieves a balance between the spicy and sweet flavor components that I love. Five-spice powder is a Chinese blend of spices incorporating the five basic flavors of Chinese cooking—savory, sweet, bitter, sour, and salty. It is available in the spice aisle of most supermarkets.

**MAKES ABOUT 1½ TABLESPOONS; ENOUGH FOR 1 BATCH OF FRIES, CHIPS, OR ONION RINGS**

2 teaspoons five-spice powder
1 teaspoon ground ginger
1 teaspoon packed light brown sugar
½ teaspoon granulated garlic
¼ teaspoon cayenne pepper

Stir together the five-spice powder, ginger, brown sugar, garlic, and cayenne in a small bowl.

# BARBECUE SEASONING

Who out there doesn't love barbecue-flavored potato chips? Toss this seasoning blend with Homemade Potato Chips (page 98) or Perfect French Fries (page 86) to satisfy your craving at home.

**MAKES ⅓ CUP; ENOUGH FOR 3 BATCHES OF FRIES, CHIPS, OR ONION RINGS**

1 tablespoon smoked sweet Spanish paprika
2 teaspoons ancho chile powder
2 teaspoons ground cumin
2 teaspoons kosher salt
1 teaspoon onion powder
1 teaspoon garlic powder
1 teaspoon packed light brown sugar
1 teaspoon freshly ground black pepper

Whisk together the paprika, ancho chile powder, cumin, salt, onion powder, garlic powder, brown sugar, and pepper in a small bowl. The seasoning will keep for up to 1 month in a tightly sealed jar in a cool, dark place.

# CUBAN SEASONING

This spice and herb blend is great for seasoning beef and turkey burgers, but I especially like it tossed with hot French fries; they are addictive! The turmeric gives fries a gorgeous golden color.

**MAKES ABOUT 2 TABLESPOONS; ENOUGH FOR 1 BATCH OF FRIES, CHIPS, OR ONION RINGS**

1 teaspoon ground bay leaves
1 teaspoon ground cumin
1 teaspoon granulated garlic
1 teaspoon granulated onion
1 teaspoon dried oregano
½ teaspoon ground turmeric

Whisk together the bay leaves, cumin, garlic, onion, oregano, and turmeric in a small bowl until combined.

# SOUTHWESTERN SEASONING

This is the seasoning mixture that I use to flavor the Southwestern fries at my Mesa Grill restaurants. It's not hot, just subtly spicy and earthy in taste. The fresh cilantro provides a bright touch of both color and flavor.

**MAKES ABOUT ¼ CUP; ENOUGH FOR 2 BATCHES OF FRIES, CHIPS, OR ONION RINGS**

1½ tablespoons ancho chile powder
1 teaspoon ground cumin
2 teaspoons kosher salt
2 tablespoons finely chopped fresh cilantro leaves

Whisk together the ancho powder, cumin, salt, and cilantro in a bowl until combined.

# MEDITERRANEAN SEASONING

Toss this seasoning mix with French fries for a perfect side dish to Mediterranean-influenced dishes or use it as a spice crust for burgers; I especially like it on turkey burgers. It also complements simply grilled chicken and fish.

**MAKES 2 TABLESPOONS; ENOUGH FOR 1 BATCH OF FRIES, CHIPS, OR ONION RINGS**

1½ teaspoons ground fennel
1½ teaspoons ground coriander
1 teaspoon dry mustard powder
1 teaspoon smoked sweet Spanish paprika
1 teaspoon dried oregano

Whisk together the fennel, coriander, mustard powder, paprika, and oregano in a small bowl until combined.

more festive, sure, but alcohol will also pump up the flavor of the milkshake's star ingredients. Or maybe it will be the star itself . . . it's hard to go wrong, either way!

When I was preparing to open Bobby's Burger Palace, we tested every last component on the menu. I figured the milkshakes would be pretty cut-and-dried . . . but boy, was I wrong! I knew what I wanted, but getting it right was another story; some were too thin, some developed an icy texture, and some just never came together: the ice cream and the milk separated as soon as the blender stopped. It turns out that the equipment you use to make your shake is as important to the final product as what you put in it! I was encountering blenders with too much speed and not enough power, so the ice cream just hovered over the blades. Instead I needed a blender with a slow, powerful blend cycle so that the ice cream could fall *into* the blades. A good blender should have extra-wide blades that are contoured to the base; this helps create a powerful vortex to draw all of the ingredients into the blade and ultimately produce a thick shake with fully integrated components.

I tried myriad blenders in the testing phase of writing this book. Many blenders I tried were good, but the models I tested from Waring and Osterizer stood out as excellent. These models quickly produced great milkshake after great milkshake, all meeting my admittedly high standards. Blenders from Waring and Osterizer (see Resources, page 156) are relatively inexpensive and are easily found in most home stores and online. For the restaurant, I found my answer in Blendtec's Total Blender. It is extremely powerful and delivers excellent results. If you are looking for a professional model and have the money to spend, I highly recommend it.

Now the only thing left is serving, and that couldn't be easier. Just pour into a chilled 10-ounce glass, add a straw, and enjoy! I have a little test for thickness, too: Does the straw stand straight up in the glass? If the answer is yes, I know I've got just what I was aiming for . . . the perfect milkshake.

# BLACKBERRY CHEESECAKE MILKSHAKE

As a native New Yorker, I grew up eating my fair share of Junior's cheesecake from Brooklyn, and I have to admit that it still continues to be one of my favorite desserts to this day. So while coming up with ideas for this chapter, I thought, cream cheese—in a milkshake? Why not? I know that strawberries are the traditional fruit topping for a cheesecake, and you can definitely use them or any other berry or fruit in the recipe, but I have a special fondness for blackberries. This milkshake is so rich, you might want to share.

**MAKES ONE 16-OUNCE MILKSHAKE OR TWO 8-OUNCE MILKSHAKES**

⅓ cup fresh fruit base made with blackberries (page 151)
¼ cup whole milk
3 ounces Philadelphia cream cheese, at room temperature
1 teaspoon grated lemon zest
9 ounces premium vanilla ice cream (about 1½ packed cups)
Fresh blackberries, for garnish

Combine the fruit base, milk, cream cheese, and lemon zest in a blender and blend until slightly smooth, about 5 seconds. Add the ice cream and blend until smooth, about 10 seconds. Serve immediately, garnished with blackberries.

**ADULTS:** Add 1 ounce (2 tablespoons) blackberry liqueur or crème de cassis to the blender when you add the fruit base.

# BLUEBERRY-POMEGRANATE MILKSHAKE

If you are craving a milkshake and still want to be able to feel somewhat virtuous, go for this shake. Blueberries and pomegranates are both proud members of the "superfoods" category and are packed with antioxidants. Of course, the main reason I use them is for their sweet yet slightly tart taste. Their fantastic color doesn't hurt, either. Thick and tangy pomegranate molasses, which is a reduction of the fruit's juice along with sugar and some form of citric acid, can be found in Middle Eastern markets and online.

**MAKES ONE 16-OUNCE MILKSHAKE OR TWO 8-OUNCE MILKSHAKES**

¼ cup fruit base made with blueberries (page 151)
3 tablespoons pomegranate molasses
¼ cup whole milk
11 ounces premium vanilla ice cream (about 1¾ packed cups)

Combine the fruit base, pomegranate molasses, and milk in a blender and blend for 5 seconds. Add the ice cream and blend until smooth, about 10 seconds. Serve immediately.

# STRAWBERRY MILKSHAKE

Simply delicious, the strawberry milkshake is an enduring favorite. I prefer to make mine with strawberry ice cream and a strawberry puree, but vanilla ice cream will work in a pinch. The sweet berry puree blends with the milk and ice cream into what looks like your standard strawberry shake, but tastes worlds better thanks to the fresh, undiluted nature of the berries.

**MAKES ONE 16-OUNCE MILKSHAKE OR TWO 8-OUNCE MILKSHAKES**

¼ cup whole milk
½ cup fruit base made with strawberries (page 151)
10 ounces premium strawberry or vanilla ice cream (about 1⅔ packed cups)
Freshly Whipped Cream (page 154)
Fresh whole strawberries, for garnish (optional)

Combine the milk and strawberry base in a blender and blend for 5 seconds. Add the ice cream and blend until smooth, about 10 seconds. Serve immediately, garnished with a dollop of whipped cream and with strawberries, if desired.

**ADULTS:** Add 1 ounce (2 tablespoons) vodka to the blender when you add the fruit base.

# BANANA-MILK CHOCOLATE CRACKLE MILKSHAKE

Crackles of chocolate are better than chips in milkshakes because they fit through the straw. You're also better off starting with bar chocolate instead of chips because the chocolate is usually of a better quality. Make sure the banana is really ripe and the chocolate is still warm when you drizzle it into the milkshake. Warm chocolate combined with the cold ice cream will instantly harden, making thin little strings of chocolate.

**MAKES ONE 16-OUNCE MILKSHAKE OR TWO 8-OUNCE MILKSHAKES**

¼ cup whole milk
1 large overly ripe banana (should have black speckles), peeled and quartered
10 ounces premium vanilla ice cream (about 1⅔ packed cups)
1 ounce milk chocolate bar (don't use chips), melted and kept warm

Combine the milk and banana in a blender and blend until slightly chunky, about 5 seconds. Add the ice cream and blend until smooth, about 10 seconds. Remove the feeder cap from the top of the lid and, with the motor running, slowly drizzle in the melted chocolate. Serve immediately.

# MOCHA-CARAMEL MILKSHAKE

This is my take on my favorite frozen coffee drink from that endlessly popular coffee chain—you know the one. As with most things, the homemade version beats the store-bought hands down. Top yours with lots of freshly whipped cream and, if you are really looking for a jolt, a smattering of chocolate-covered espresso beans, and the mass-market variety doesn't stand a chance.

**MAKES ONE 16-OUNCE MILKSHAKE OR
TWO 8-OUNCE MILKSHAKES**

¼ cup whole milk
½ teaspoon instant espresso powder
3 tablespoons Chocolate Syrup (page 153)
3 tablespoons Caramel Sauce (page 153),
    plus more for garnish
11 ounces premium coffee ice cream
    (about 1¾ packed cups)
Freshly Whipped Cream (page 154)
Chocolate-covered espresso beans,
    for garnish (optional)

Combine the milk, espresso powder, chocolate syrup, and caramel sauce in a blender and blend for 5 seconds. Add the ice cream and blend until smooth, about 10 seconds. Serve immediately, garnished with whipped cream and chocolate-covered espresso beans and a drizzle of caramel sauce, if desired.

**ADULTS:** Add 1 ounce (2 tablespoons) Kahlúa to the blender when you add the milk.

# VANILLA COCONUT MILKSHAKE

This milkshake is so simple but so incredibly amazing and rich. I put this on the menu at Bobby's Burger Palace and I have one every time I am there.

**MAKES ONE 16-OUNCE MILKSHAKE OR TWO 8-OUNCE MILKSHAKES**

¼ cup whole milk
⅓ cup cream of coconut, such as Coco López
11 ounces premium vanilla ice cream (about 1¾ packed cups)
Toasted dried shredded sweetened coconut, for garnish (optional)

Combine the milk and cream of coconut in a blender and blend for 5 seconds. Add the ice cream and blend until smooth, about 10 seconds. Serve immediately, garnished with toasted coconut, if desired.

## PIÑA COLADA MILKSHAKE

Add ¼ cup chopped fresh pineapple and 1 ounce (2 tablespoons) dark rum or coconut rum when you blend together the milk and cream of coconut.

# DOUBLE CHOCOLATE MILKSHAKE

What could be better than a chocolate milkshake? A double chocolate milkshake made with premium chocolate ice cream *and* chocolate syrup. You can turn this into a malted by adding the malt powder or into a chocolate soda milkshake by adding a splash of seltzer water.

**MAKES ONE 16-OUNCE MILKSHAKE OR TWO 8-OUNCE MILKSHAKES**

⅓ cup whole milk
3 tablespoons Chocolate Syrup (page 153)
2 tablespoons malt powder (optional)
11 ounces premium chocolate ice cream (about 1¾ packed cups)
"Fluffy" Whipped Cream (page 154; optional)

Combine the milk, chocolate syrup, and malt powder, if using, in a blender and blend for 5 seconds. Add the ice cream and blend until smooth, about 10 seconds. Serve immediately, topped with a dollop of fluffy whipped cream, if desired.

# BLACK AND WHITE MILKSHAKE

A black and white milkshake is a chocolate milkshake made with vanilla ice cream and chocolate syrup. Think of this as a more delicate version of a chocolate milkshake.

**MAKES ONE 16-OUNCE MILKSHAKE OR TWO 8-OUNCE MILKSHAKES**

⅓ cup whole milk
¼ cup Chocolate Syrup (page 153)
11 ounces premium vanilla ice cream (about 1¾ packed cups)

Combine the milk and chocolate sauce in a blender and blend for 5 seconds. Add the ice cream and blend until smooth, about 10 seconds. Serve immediately.

# TOASTED ALMOND MILKSHAKE

I love the nuttiness and crunchiness that toasted and chopped almonds add to this milkshake. Just a tiny drop of almond extract is needed to enhance the flavor of the nuts; it should veer toward subtle as opposed to overwhelming. Though the basic recipe is delicious as is, you can also take some liberties, and I have given a couple of suggestions for doing so below. I am partial to the Chocolate Almond Coconut Milkshake, which tastes just like one of my favorite candy bars.

**MAKES ONE 16-OUNCE MILKSHAKE OR TWO 8-OUNCE MILKSHAKES**

- ½ cup plus 1 tablespoon coarsely chopped almonds, lightly toasted
- ¾ cup whole milk
- 1 tablespoon sugar
- ¼ teaspoon pure almond extract
- 11 ounces premium vanilla ice cream (about 1¾ packed cups)
- Freshly Whipped Cream (page 154; optional)

**1.** Combine ½ cup of the almonds, the milk, and the sugar in a small saucepan and bring to a simmer over medium heat. Transfer to a bowl, cover, and let steep in the refrigerator for at least 4 hours.

**2.** Strain the milk into a blender (discard the nuts). Add the almond extract and ice cream and blend until smooth, about 10 seconds. Serve immediately, topped with a dollop of whipped cream, if desired, and garnished with the remaining 1 tablespoon chopped almonds.

**ADULTS:** Add 1 ounce (2 tablespoons) Amaretto liqueur to the blender.

## CHOCOLATE ALMOND MILKSHAKE

Substitute chocolate ice cream for the vanilla ice cream.

## CHOCOLATE ALMOND COCONUT MILKSHAKE

Substitute chocolate ice cream for the vanilla, and add 3 tablespoons cream of coconut.

# DARK CHOCOLATE MILKSHAKE WITH "FLUFFY" COCONUT CREAM

This is my homage to what I consider to be one of the best candy bars on the planet: Fran's Coconut Gold Bar created by Fran's Chocolates in Seattle, Washington. The bar consists of bittersweet chocolate wrapped around a creamy coconut–white chocolate ganache center. It's off-the-charts good! To achieve that contrast between the bitter dark chocolate and the sweet coconut ganache in a milkshake, I combine a double chocolate shake with a mousse-like coconut whipped cream and layer this shake like a parfait. All you need to do is dig in your straw and stir for a little bit of heaven.

**MAKES ONE 16-OUNCE MILKSHAKE**

¼ cup plus 2 tablespoons heavy cream
3 tablespoons cream of coconut, such as Coco López
2 tablespoons Marshmallow Fluff
⅓ cup whole milk
3 tablespoons Chocolate Syrup (page 153)
11 ounces premium chocolate ice cream (about 1¾ packed cups)
Toasted dried shredded sweetened coconut, for garnish (optional)

**1.** Combine the heavy cream, cream of coconut, and Marshmallow Fluff in a medium bowl. Using a hand-held mixer, whip until stiff peaks form.

**2.** Combine the milk and chocolate syrup in a blender and blend for 5 seconds. Add the ice cream and blend until smooth, about 10 seconds. Pour one-third of the milkshake into a 16-ounce glass and top with ¼ cup of the coconut cream mixture. Repeat with another third of the milkshake and ¼ cup coconut cream. Top with the remaining third of the milkshake. Top with the remaining 2 tablespoons coconut cream and garnish with toasted coconut, if desired. Serve immediately.

# FRESH MINT-CHOCOLATE SPECKLED MILKSHAKE

I like mint–chocolate chip ice cream, but I think this shake with the same combination of flavors hits it out of the park. Even forgetting the scary, unnatural green color, most commercial mint ice creams taste a touch artificial. Steeping fresh mint leaves in milk and adding that to vanilla ice cream perfumes the shake with a bold yet refreshing mintiness. This recipe makes enough mint-flavored milk for two 16-ounce shakes (or four 8-ounce shakes). If you're going to go to the trouble, you may as well make enough to share. The milk will keep for several days in the refrigerator. I have never liked the way chocolate chips mix—or, rather, *don't* mix—into shakes. You can never get the pieces through your straw! I speckle this shake with chocolate by slowly pouring warm melted chocolate into the whirring blender; when it hits the cold ice cream mixture, the chocolate hardens into small drinkable flakes.

**MAKES ONE 16-OUNCE MILKSHAKE OR TWO 8-OUNCE MILKSHAKES**

1 cup whole milk
1 cup coarsely chopped fresh mint leaves plus 4 whole mint leaves and additional sprigs, for garnish (optional)
2 tablespoons sugar
11 ounces premium vanilla ice cream (about 1¾ packed cups)
1 ounce bittersweet chocolate bar (don't use chips), melted and kept warm

**1.** Combine the milk, chopped mint leaves, and sugar in a small saucepan and bring to a simmer. Transfer to a bowl, cover, and refrigerate for at least 8 hours and up to 24 hours. Strain the milk into a bowl.

**2.** Pour ½ cup of the mint-flavored milk into a blender (reserve the remaining ½ cup milk for another shake), add the whole mint leaves, and blend for 5 seconds. Add the ice cream and blend until almost smooth, about 7 seconds. With the motor running, slowly pour the melted chocolate through the feed tube on the lid of the blender and blend for 5 seconds. Serve immediately, garnished with mint sprigs, if desired.

**ADULTS:** Add 1 ounce (2 tablespoons) crème de menthe to the blender when you add the mint-flavored milk.

## CHOCOLATE-CHOCOLATE MINT SHAKE

Substitute chocolate ice cream for the vanilla ice cream.

# LEMON MERINGUE PIE MILKSHAKE

A perfectly baked golden buttery crust filled with rich lemon custard and topped with a light and fluffy meringue is pretty much heaven. Well, now you can have your pie and drink it, too. Top this one off with a large dollop of "Fluffy" Whipped Cream and garnish it with a vanilla cookie for crunch. Yum! Are you in the mood for a Key lime pie? Substitute Key lime curd, lime zest, and lime juice for the lemon.

**MAKES ONE 16-OUNCE MILKSHAKE OR TWO 8-OUNCE MILKSHAKES**

¼ cup whole milk
1 tablespoon grated lemon zest, plus more, for garnish (optional)
2 tablespoons fresh lemon juice
3 heaping tablespoons store-bought lemon curd
11 ounces premium vanilla ice cream (about 1¾ packed cups)
"Fluffy" Whipped Cream (page 154)
Pizzelle cookie, for garnish (optional)

Combine the milk, lemon zest, lemon juice, and lemon curd in a blender and blend for 5 seconds. Add the ice cream and blend until smooth, about 10 seconds. Top the shake with fluffy whipped cream, some lemon zest, and a pizzelle cookie, if desired. Serve immediately.

BOBBY
FLAY'S
BURGERS,
FRIES &
SHAKES

142

# PEACH BELLINI MILKSHAKE

Every time I visit Venice, Italy, one of my first stops is Cipriani for their signature Bellini cocktail, a wonderful mixture of fresh peach puree topped with cold sparkling Champagne. To make my milkshake version kid-friendly, just top it off with a splash of seltzer water.

**MAKES ONE 16-OUNCE MILKSHAKE OR TWO 8-OUNCE MILKSHAKES**

¼ cup whole milk
1 cup coarsely chopped peeled very ripe fresh peaches or thawed frozen peaches
2 tablespoons sugar
10 ounces premium vanilla ice cream (about 1⅔ packed cups)
Champagne or sparkling wine, chilled
Fresh peach slice, for garnish (optional)

Combine the milk, chopped peaches, and sugar in a blender and blend until coarsely pureed, about 5 seconds. Add the ice cream and blend until smooth, about 10 seconds. Pour into a 16-ounce glass, leaving 1 inch at the top. Top off with Champagne and garnish with a fresh peach slice, if desired. Serve immediately.

# PEANUT BUTTER-BANANA-MARSHMALLOW MILKSHAKE

I am one of the few people whose mother never packed a Fluffernutter sandwich in their school lunch box. You know what? That's okay. The thought of peanut butter, marshmallow, and banana "sandwiched" between two slices of squishy, flavorless bread was not so appetizing to me even as a child. However, when you get rid of the bread and add some ice cream and milk to those three ingredients, it's a totally different story. If only my mom had filled my lunch-box thermos with this shake.

**MAKES ONE 16-OUNCE MILKSHAKE OR**
**TWO 8-OUNCE MILKSHAKES**

½ cup whole milk
1 medium overly ripe banana (should have black speckles), peeled and quartered
3 heaping tablespoons creamy peanut butter (do not use natural)
3 heaping tablespoons Marshmallow Fluff
10 ounces premium vanilla ice cream (about 1⅔ packed cups)

Combine the milk, banana, peanut butter, and Marshmallow Fluff in a blender and blend until combined, about 7 seconds. Add the ice cream and blend until smooth, about 10 seconds. Serve immediately.

# ROASTED PINEAPPLE MILKSHAKE

This might be one of the more esoteric shakes in this book, but I hope you find it intriguing, not off-putting. The extra step of roasting the pineapple is well worth your time. Roasting concentrates the pineapple's flavor and intensifies its sweetness as the heat of the oven caramelizes the fruit's natural sugars. Tart lemon sorbet is added to balance that sweetness and for its icy texture. Using pineapple juice gives this shake a depth of flavor and refreshing quality that milk wouldn't provide.

**MAKES FOUR 6-OUNCE MILKSHAKES**

½ small ripe Golden pineapple, core removed, cut into wedges (3 cups)
½ cup pineapple juice, chilled
¼ cup lemon sorbet
10 ounces premium vanilla ice cream (about 1⅔ packed cups)
Seltzer water

**1.** Preheat the oven to 375 degrees F.

**2.** Combine the pineapple and ¼ cup of the juice in a small roasting dish and roast in the oven, turning once, until golden brown, about 15 minutes. Remove from the oven and let cool completely.

**3.** Set aside 4 pineapple wedges for garnish. Put the remaining cooled roasted pineapple, any juice from the roasting dish, and the remaining ¼ cup pineapple juice in a blender and blend until combined, about 7 seconds. Add the sorbet and ice cream and blend until smooth, about 10 seconds. Serve in 4 large wine goblets and top each with a splash of seltzer and a pineapple wedge.

**ADULTS:** Add 2 ounces (¼ cup) dark rum to the blender when you add the pineapple.

# TOASTED MARSHMALLOW MILKSHAKE

Don't laugh . . . it works, and it's good. The key is to make sure that your marshmallows are really toasted to a deep golden brown color on all sides to get the most flavor. Don't walk away from the oven because the marshmallows brown quickly. Would a dollop of "Fluffy" Whipped Cream (page 154) on top be overkill? I think not! In the mood for S'mores? Just blend the toasted marshmallows into the Double Chocolate Milkshake (page 134) and add a few tablespoons of crushed graham crackers on top of the whipped cream.

**MAKES ONE 16-OUNCE MILKSHAKE OR TWO 8-OUNCE MILKSHAKES**

Nonstick cooking spray
9 large marshmallows
¼ cup whole milk
11 ounces premium vanilla ice cream
   (about 1¾ packed cups)
Toasted marshmallows, for garnish (optional)

**1.** Preheat the broiler. Line a rimmed baking sheet with parchment paper and spray with nonstick cooking spray.

**2.** Arrange the marshmallows flat on the baking sheet and place under the broiler until the tops are a deep golden brown color, about 40 seconds. Remove from the oven, carefully turn the marshmallows over, and broil until they are deep golden brown. Remove from the oven and let cool slightly.

**3.** Combine the marshmallows and milk in a blender and blend for 5 seconds. Add the ice cream and blend until smooth, about 10 seconds. Serve immediately.

# VANILLA BEAN MILKSHAKE

What can I say about this one? Sometimes the best things in life are the simplest, and a thick and creamy vanilla milkshake is definitely one of those things. The fresh vanilla bean will give you a shake flecked with tiny dark specks of recognizable vanilla, but its true and intense flavor is a quality far greater than cosmetic. Basic but never boring, the vanilla shake can also be doctored up in dozens of ways. I've included a couple of my favorite variations below.

**MAKES ONE 16-OUNCE MILKSHAKE OR TWO 8-OUNCE MILKSHAKES**

½ cup whole milk
½ fresh vanilla bean, split and seeds
    scraped (reserve the pod for another use)
11 ounces premium vanilla ice cream (about
    1¾ packed cups)

Combine the milk and vanilla bean seeds in a blender and blend until combined, about 5 seconds. Add the ice cream and blend until smooth, about 10 seconds.

**ADULTS:** Add 1 ounce (2 tablespoons) bourbon to the blender when you add the milk.

### SPICED VANILLA BEAN MILKSHAKE

Add ¼ teaspoon ground cinnamon and ⅛ teaspoon ground nutmeg.

### VANILLA BEAN-CARAMEL MILKSHAKE

Decrease the milk to ¼ cup and add ¼ cup Caramel Sauce (page 153).

# FRESH FRUIT BASE

When we were testing milkshake recipes for Bobby's Burger Palace, I learned some interesting things about fruit-based milkshakes, especially about milkshakes made with fresh berries: Berries are very expensive. Berries are extremely perishable. Berries are inconsistent in taste (ranging from sweet to tart) and texture (ranging from watery to dense). All these factors presented a problem when we were trying to create a thick, flavorful milkshake. We needed to find an alternative, still using fresh fruit, that would produce a consistently thick and flavorful milkshake every single time.

We found a company on Long Island that produces fresh fruit purees. The purees are thick and almost jam-like in texture, and they add incredible fresh fruit flavor while not compromising the thickness of the shake. Now the recipe from the company that produces the purees for us is top secret, but I have created something very close to make at home. In addition to providing a wonderful fresh fruit flavor, these bases will also keep in the refrigerator or freezer for a good amount of time—unlike fresh berries, which tend to go bad in a few days. Just add ¼ cup or so to vanilla or chocolate ice cream for an intensely good shake.

**MAKES ABOUT 1¼ CUPS**

1 pound fresh strawberries, blueberries, blackberries, or raspberries, or a mixture
4 to 6 tablespoons sugar (depending on sweetness of the berries)
3 tablespoons strawberry, blueberry, blackberry, or raspberry jam
2 teaspoons fresh lemon juice

**1.** Put the berries in a bowl (hull strawberries), add 3 tablespoons sugar, and gently stir to combine. Let the berries sit at room temperature for 30 minutes, or until they start to soften and release their juices.

**2.** Transfer the mixture to a medium nonreactive saucepan, add the jam, and cook over medium-high heat until slightly softened. Coarsely mash the berries using a potato masher or the back of a fork and continue cooking, stirring occasionally, until the mixture thickens to a jam-like consistency, about 20 minutes.

**3.** Remove from the heat and stir in the lemon juice. Taste the mixture and add the remaining 1 tablespoon sugar, if needed, stirring to dissolve. Transfer to a bowl and let cool. Cover and refrigerate until cold and thickened, at least 2 hours or up to 24 hours. The fruit base can be frozen (in ¼-cup portions, if desired) for up to 6 months. Defrost in the refrigerator overnight before using.

# CHOCOLATE SYRUP

I like making my own chocolate syrup because I can control the sweetness and the quality of the cocoa powder. Plus, it couldn't be simpler.
**MAKES 1¹/₂ CUPS**

½ cup sugar
1 tablespoon light corn syrup
⅔ cup unsweetened good-quality Dutch-processed cocoa powder, such as Ghirardelli or Valrhona
1 teaspoon pure vanilla extract

Bring 1 cup water, the sugar, and the corn syrup to a boil in a small saucepan over high heat. Whisk in the cocoa powder and cook until the mixture is slightly thickened, about 2 minutes. Remove from the heat and whisk in the vanilla. Transfer to a bowl and let cool to room temperature. Store covered in the refrigerator for up to 1 week.

# CARAMEL SAUCE

You won't find any caramel sauce like this at your local market. Letting the sugar cook until it reaches a deep amber color gives this sauce an incredibly rich flavor that really holds up in your shake. Adding a few tablespoons of dark rum will only intensify the flavor, but if you are serving it to kids or alcohol isn't your thing, leave it out . . . the sauce will still be amazing.
**MAKES ABOUT 1 CUP**

1½ cups sugar
¾ cup heavy cream
2 tablespoons dark rum (optional)
½ teaspoon pure vanilla extract

**1.** Combine the sugar and ¼ cup water in a medium saucepan and bring to a boil over high heat, swirling the pot occasionally (do not stir) to even out the color. Cook until deep amber in color, 10 to 12 minutes.

**2.** While the caramel is cooking, pour the heavy cream into a small saucepan and bring to a simmer over medium heat. Remove from the heat and keep warm.

**3.** When the caramel has reached a deep amber color, slowly whisk in the heavy cream. Be careful; the hot mixture will bubble. Whisk until smooth. Remove from the heat and stir in the rum, if using, and the vanilla extract. The sauce can be cooled, covered, and refrigerated for up to 1 week. Reheat over low heat or in the microwave. Serve warm.

# FRESHLY WHIPPED CREAM

This is a basic recipe for making your own freshly whipped cream. You can halve, double, or triple this recipe depending on how many milkshakes you are making. Figure on about ¼ cup per shake. Also, you can add other flavorings and extracts. Just make sure that the heavy cream is really cold to get the best volume.

**MAKES ABOUT 3 CUPS**

1 cup heavy cream
2 tablespoons sugar
½ teaspoon pure vanilla extract

Combine the cream, sugar, and vanilla in a large bowl and whip until soft peaks form. The whipped cream can be made 1 hour in advance and stored, covered, in the refrigerator. Whisk slightly before using.

# "FLUFFY" WHIPPED CREAM

The addition of Marshmallow Fluff gives this a mousse-like consistency and makes it the perfect topping for the Lemon Meringue Pie Milkshake (page 141), Double Chocolate Milkshake (134), and Peanut Butter–Banana–Marshmallow Milkshake (page 145).

**MAKES ABOUT 3 CUPS**

1 cup heavy cream
1 tablespoon sugar
¼ cup Marshmallow Fluff
½ teaspoon pure vanilla extract

Combine the cream, sugar, Fluff, and vanilla in a large bowl and whip until soft peaks form. The whipped cream can be made 2 hours in advance and stored, covered, in the refrigerator. Whisk slightly before using.

# RESOURCES

**Spices**
www.kalustyans.com
www.penzeys.com

Bobby Flay Spice Rubs, BBQ Sauce, and Hot Sauce
www.bobbyflay.com

**Cheese**
www.murrayscheese.com

**Cast-Iron Pans, Grill Pans, and Griddles**
Bobby Flay line at www.kohls.com
www.lodgemfg.com

**Blenders and Deep Fryers**
www.waringproducts.com
www.oster.com

**Basting Covers, Metal Spatulas,
and Spiders**
www.cooking.com

# ACKNOWLEDGMENTS

Stephanie Banyas, Sally Jackson, Renee Forsberg, J. C. Pavlovich, Bobby Mundell, Laurence Kretchmer, Manny Gatdula, Jennifer Lee, Alexia Fimmano, Beth Leakway, Maggie Jackson, Bella Sirugio, Ben Fink, Lauren Shakely, Marysarah Quinn, Selina Cicogna, Chris Tanigawa, Mary Rodgers, Jenny Coleman, Maria Salazar, Food Network, Kohl's ✱ The staffs at Mesa Grill NYC, Mesa Grill Las Vegas, Mesa Grill Bahamas, Bar Americain, Bobby Flay Steak, and Bobby's Burger Palace ✱ A special thank-you to my amazing editor, Rica Allannic, for her hard work, dedication, and support.